THE
DAVINCI
DECEPTION

100 Questions about the Facts and Fiction of *The DaVinci Code*

By Mark Shea, Edward Sri, S.T.D., and
the Editors of Catholic Exchange

ASCENSION PRESS
West Chester, PA

Catholic Exchange
Your Faith · Your Life · Your World
Encinitas, CA

Scripture verses contained herein are from the Catholic
Edition of the *Revised Standard Version* of the Bible, copyright
1965, 1966 by the Division of Christian Education of the
National Council of the Churches of Christ in the United
States of America. Used by permission.

Ascension Press
Post Office Box 1990
West Chester, PA 19380
Orders: 1-800-376-0520
www.AscensionPress.com

Cover design: Devin Schadt

Printed in the United States of America

ISBN 1-932927-64-6

CONTENTS

INTRODUCTION

I t's certainly no secret that we live in a media culture, one that impacts the way we perceive the world around us. A well-made movie, an engaging novel, or a beautiful painting can create an entirely new world and draw us into it. Art has the power to help us think and feel our way to the heart of what it means to be human.

Given the profound power of art to touch us at the most subliminal and fundamental levels of our psyches, we need to approach it with a discerning spirit, a critical eye. A skilled artist without a conscience can pervert his or her gifts to dreadful ends. An infamous example from the past century is Leni Reifenstahl's 1935 film *Triumph of the Will*. Considered simply as an exercise in the art of filmmaking, *Triumph of the Will* is widely acknowledged as a towering technical achievement. To this day, it retains its hypnotic power to move the viewer with the sheer grandiosity of its spectacle. And yet all the skill and expertise in creating this film had as its end the exaltation of Adolf Hitler and the glorification of the Nazi state. *Triumph of the Will* is the cinematic equivalent of a Renaissance master painter using all his skill to create a vivid and strangely attractive portrait of a dung heap. Worse still, this insidious film did a masterful job persuading countless people of the glory of the Nazi cause and thereby contributed to the deaths of millions.

Art has a gigantic power to persuade—and deceive. And this becomes only more potent as we enter an age in which fewer and fewer people get their information from books and are more and more at the mercy of whatever images a filmmaker chooses to show them. Many filmmakers and writers are true artists who seek to use their unique gifts to portray that which is true, good, and beautiful. But not a few are simply skilled technicians who know how to manipulate a crowd. Such are not "artists" at all—they are propagandists, much like Reifenstahl.

Dan Brown, the author of *The Da Vinci Code*, seems to fall into this category. While some may take offense at calling Brown a "propagandist," an even cursory familiarity with the content of the book is sufficient evidence to back up this claim. *The Da Vinci Code* is the epitome of the old saying that if you are going to tell a lie, make it a really big one since people seem to believe big lies much more easily than small ones. It skillfully taps into what one author has called "America's last acceptable prejudice"—anti-Catholicism—and it has wooed and intimidated more than 30 million readers with its combination of mysterious puzzles, phony erudition, bogus history, conspiracy-theorizing, and, above all, relentless and deliberate lies about the Catholic Church and the Christian Gospel.

I wish I could soften that language a bit and say that Dan Brown is simply "mistaken" about the Church. But that would not be honest. Brown knows exactly what he is doing. He has a deep hostility to the Christian Gospel and to the Catholic Church in particular and fills his novel not merely with mistakes but with malicious lies with one end in view: to attack the Gospel of Jesus Christ and replace it with a resurgent pagan mythos. Along the way, he smears Catholics as mass murderers, and tells bald-faced lies about the Council of Nicea, the origins of the Bible, and Jesus' supposed "transformation" into God at the hands of the early Church. He sets out a blizzard of phony "facts" about history, art, religion, theology, and Western culture. He intimidates with fake erudition, gets even easily verifiable facts embarrassingly wrong, claims to celebrate the "sacred feminine" while subjecting his heroine to endless lectures from two men who condescend to fill her pretty little head with the Hidden Knowledge of the Truth, and, to be brief, tells rank lies under the guise of writing "fiction" for one main purpose: to fix in the reader's mind the conviction that "everything our fathers taught us about Christ is *false*."

This claim is at the very heart of *The Da Vinci Code*. It is the reason it is interesting to so many. Virtually nobody who reads the book is interested in its dull, two-dimensional characters who largely consist of the Lecturers and the Lectured (with a smattering of the Murderers and the Murdered on the side). Nobody much cares for the rudimentary twists and turns of this standard thriller, with its narrow escapes, contrived "clues," and so forth. What has gripped people's imaginations is simply this: Is Christianity one gigantic and audacious lie? Has all of Western civilization been founded on the biggest fraud in history? Could it be?

We need to be aware that Brown provides no actual evidence for his attacks on the Faith. Search where you will throughout the fogbank of bogus facts, dimestore erudition, naked lies, and tendentious arguments, and you will find not a single actual fact that overturns the basic claims of the Gospel, much less establishes Brown's "alternative history" or silly attempts to establish a neo-pagan religion with Jesus as Hippie-in-Chief, worshiping his girlfriend while his jealous buddies gripe about her like Beatles resentful of Yoko Ono.

Fiction is great when it is told in order to speak the truth. Fiction is perverted and evil when it is told in order to speak lies. And the answer to such deception is what it has always been: truth. *The Da Vinci Code*—the Dan Brown novel and now the Ron Howard/Tom Hanks film extravaganza—urges us to "Seek the Truth." As Catholics, we have absolutely no fear of this exhortation—and the book you are holding in your hands is the proof. For we have complete confidence in Christ, the Incarnate God, whose voice speaks in all ages and assures us that "If you continue in my word, you are truly my disciples, and you will know the truth, and the truth will make you free" (John 8:31-32).

> — Tom Allen
> President and Editor-in-Chief
> *CatholicExchange.com*
> January 19, 2006

CHAPTER 1

THE NOVEL, THE AUTHOR, AND WHY THEY MATTER

1. What is *The Da Vinci Code?*

The Da Vinci Code is a best-selling novel by Dan Brown that claims the Catholic Church has suppressed the truth about Jesus by covering up the fact that He married Mary Magdalene and meant to establish the worship of "the sacred feminine," not a Church that worships Him as the Son of God.

According to *Code*, Mary Magdalene is the true "holy Grail" (traditionally held to be the cup used by Christ at the Last Supper) since it was her womb that held the "sacred blood" of Jesus as she gave birth to a bloodline that would eventually become the Merovingian Dynasty, a medieval family of French kings. The central claim of the novel is that this was known to a secret society that kept the truth alive over the centuries, despite the sinister schemes of the Catholic Church to suppress the truth. Leonardo da Vinci, it is alleged, was in on this dark secret and revealed it in a series of secret codes encrypted into his paintings.

The Da Vinci Code has more than 35 million copies in print and has been made into a major motion picture. Because of its radical claims about the allegedly fraudulent origins of the Christian faith, the book has been at the center of intense controversy—a controversy that can and should be addressed by Christians.

2. **But isn't the book just fiction? Dan Brown might not be able to get his facts straight, but he sure tells a great story. What's the harm in people reading this as a thrilling novel?**

The Da Vinci Code exploits people's lack of knowledge about Scripture, history, and the Catholic faith, and its "facts" mislead them in many harmful ways.

First, it gives ammunition—however ungrounded in reality it may be—to people who already hold a grudge against Christianity. In other words, people who already distrust (and even dislike) the Catholic Church and traditional Christianity are likely to see in *The Da Vinci Code* much "evidence" to help justify their opposition to the Church and to support their own views about Christ.

Second, *The Da Vinci Code* gives Christians who are on the fence about their faith an excuse for not following Jesus Christ unreservedly. Those people, for example, who may have grown up Christian but have not been fully living out their relationship with Jesus in their personal lives are encouraged by *The Da Vinci Code* to continue in their lukewarm lifestyle.

Third, *The Da Vinci Code* draws all readers—even devout Christians—emotionally and intellectually into many levels of conspiracy theories in a way that is unhealthy. Many die-hard, believing Christians who have read the novel have commented on how disturbing many of the book's ideas are and how, once those ideas were planted in the minds, their faith was shaken. The conspiracy theories in *The Da Vinci Code* get us to approach the Holy Bible, the Catholic Church, and Sacred Tradition with much suspicion. We must ask ourselves: Do we want this kind of attitude in our hearts? Does *Christ* want us to have this kind of attitude? Do we want to approach Christ and the Church with a lack of trust? Do we want to come to God's Word in the Bible with many doubts about its credibility?

Let's keep in mind who the very first conspiracy theorist was. The one who, from the very beginning, sowed doubt about God's goodness in the human heart. Who is it that still wants us to doubt God's Scriptures, God's Church, God's law, and even God Himself? The devil. It was the devil who led Adam and Eve to doubt God's love and good intentions: "Did God say, 'you shall not eat of any tree of the garden'? ...You will not die! For God knows that when you eat of it your eyes will be opened, and you will be like God" (Genesis 3:1, 4-5). So yes, the many conspiracy theories woven in *The Da Vinci Code* can be very dangerous for the soul.

3. **Aren't Christians scared of *The Da Vinci Code* because they know Dan Brown has discovered the truth about the fraudulent origins of their faith? The book seems to be rooted in good research and historical facts.**

One of the ironies of *The Da Vinci Code* is the curious way in which so many of its defenders say, "Lighten up, it's just a novel! And besides—it's all true!" We will leave it to you to work out that self-contradiction. In the meantime, we will counter the book's claims with a straightforward fact: They're not true.

True, *The Da Vinci Code* is just a novel, but it gives the impression that its contents are based on historical truth. Indeed, the very first page of the book has a list of supposed facts, including this statement: "All descriptions of artwork, architecture, documents and secret rituals in this novel are accurate." So, right off the bat, the author wants readers to believe they are encountering much more than fiction in *Code;* that there are many authentic claims made about religious documents, art, and rituals in the midst of its story line.

Also, many advertisements and much media attention given to *The Da Vinci Code* portray the book as being "historically researched," "based on historical facts," "an historical novel," or "based on impeccable research." The very slogan for the film version of *The Da Vinci Code* is "Seek the Truth." And experts in the publishing trade say the book is so successful because it combines historical facts with a contemporary plot. But that's the problem: Many people think they are getting a lot of facts and history, but in reality, many of the central points made in the book are *not* factual. Scholars in the fields of history, art, theology, and Scripture have noted that the book is not at all based on solid research. In fact, a number of the claims made in *The Da Vinci Code* are as easily disproved as claims that "the earth is flat" or "2+2=5." However, the average American—i.e., someone who does not know much about the Bible, early Christian history, or religious symbolism—might buy into the bizarre ideas in *The Da Vinci Code* because he or she does not have the background to separate the truth from the many falsehoods found in its pages.

After all, how many people are experts in first-century Judaism? In early Christian history? In religious art? In the Bible? So when a professional "expert" character in *The Da Vinci Code* starts quoting ancient documents you've never heard of, or begins spouting off "scholarly" theories about how there were more than eighty gospels used in the early Church, or declares that Christ's marriage to Mary Magdalene is a matter of historical record, or tells you there is no evidence in the first three centuries of Christians believing that Jesus is God, the reaction of the intimidated reader is "What do I know? Maybe *The Da Vinci Code* is right!" Many readers who are not well-educated in these areas are easily taken for a ride. They begin to wonder whether maybe, just maybe, some of the points Brown makes in *The Da Vinci Code* could be true after all. Especially when the book backs up its claims by asserting that "scholars," "historians," and "educated Christians" all know this stuff. The average lay person does not feel informed enough to make an intelligent rebuttal, so many believe *The Da Vinci Code's* pseudo-history.

4. **Isn't the fact that the book has sold millions of copies a testament to its truth and credibility?**

Just because something is popular or makes a lot of money for its creator(s) does not mean it is a good thing. For example, pornography makes more money than the NFL, NBA, NHL, and Major League Baseball. But few would say that pornography's tremendous financial success (and, alas, its popularity) proves that it is good.

In other words, the phenomenal sales of a book such as *The Da Vinci Code* are more a sign of a broken culture than they are evidence of the credibility of its claims. If people knew more about the Bible, Church history, and the Catholic faith, most would realize that many of the points made in *The Da Vinci Code* are downright silly and very far removed from reality. Yet millions of people have been led to believe this book would teach them much about history and religion. It's like buying a new, good-looking car that happens to have its engine missing. It may be great to look at, but it's not going to get you very far. Similarly, *The Da Vinci Code* might be a fun, exciting read for some people, but it's certainly not the kind of book that makes people more educated. In fact, it's the kind of book that actually makes people less knowledgeable and more confused about history, art, and religion than they were before they read it.

5.   **Why is *The Da Vinci Code* so popular anyway?**

The book is popular not because the characters are interesting or even because the plot is very well constructed, but because it claims to be revealing a huge secret: the fraudulent origins of Christianity. The curious thing about this outrageous claim is that Brown cannot make up his mind about the *basis* of this claim. Throughout the book, we are simultaneously told that this is *the* gigantic secret of the ages: the one thing the colossal Roman Catholic conspiracy has stopped at nothing to suppress through murder, chicanery, and intrigue for 2,000 years. But, on the other hand, we are also told that this is common knowledge to "serious scholars," something that anyone who "opens his eyes" can see at any time. Indeed, the whole book revolves around the notion that Leonardo da Vinci was just one in a number of European elites who knew of Jesus' marriage and child, and who sneered at the thought that He was the Son of God.

Despite the fact that the entire apparatus of the evil Roman Church was ready to murder anybody who let out the secret, Leonardo was busily telling the world through cleverly encoded artwork painted on the walls of Catholic churches! It's this titillating—and fundamentally self-contradictory—proposition that is the underlying interest of the book. The characters are simply mouthpieces for instructing the reader in this baseless claim.

6.   Who is Dan Brown?

Dan Brown is the author of several detective thrillers that generally involve the untangling of an elaborate web of lies and intrigue in the quest for what film director Alfred Hitchcock called the *maguffin*: the object that is the goal of the pursuit throughout the story. A 1986 graduate of Amherst College, Brown taught English at Phillips Exeter Academy (of which he is an alumnus and where his father taught math). Upon finishing a pulp fiction novel one day, Brown reportedly said, "I could do that." So he embarked on a career as a full-time writer, cranking out a number of novels that would recycle his interest in and ideas about codes, keys, and secret information. Despite the fact that Brown has no training in history, art, theology, philosophy, or even cryptography, he makes a special claim to meticulously research his work, a claim that had been repeatedly challenged long before the debut of *The Da Vinci Code*.

For instance, his novel *Digital Fortress* earned scorn for its erroneous depiction of cryptography—a rather crucial fault since the book is *about* cryptography. Similarly, Brown has been criticized for his confident—and wholly invented—claims in *Digital Fortress* that, in Spain, the "hospitals smell of urine," the police "can be easily bribed," and "making an international call depends on how lucky you are." He writes of one of his wounded characters that "such a lung injury could be easily treated in any medically advanced nation, but this was Spain." Consequently, the mayor of Seville (the Spanish city where the novel is partially set) invited Brown to visit the city so that he might know what he's talking about.

As we have mentioned, Brown's tendency to make extremely dubious claims with great confidence is on particular display in *The Da Vinci Code*. In a whole host of areas—including art, history, theology, and architecture—Brown makes a number of highly questionable assertions concerning not only the "fraudulent origins" of the Christian faith, but about art and history as well.

7. **Why does the book begin with a "statement of facts"?**

Because Brown wants the reader to believe that he has done his homework. The problem is that even his "FACT" page is full of errors! Here, we will consider just one of these "facts"—his claims about Opus Dei.

Brown says that some members of Opus Dei practice "corporal mortification." Our guide to this practice throughout the book is Silas, a hulking albino monk who takes masochistic pleasure inflicting himself with bloody wounds. We are, of course, expected to do the math: Opus Dei = sick and sinister cult.

What Brown doesn't tell you is that "corporal mortification" is not a practice unique to Christians, much less Catholics or Opus Dei (whose mortifications are vastly tamer affairs than the lurid nonsense of Brown's imagination). Indeed, corporal mortification is not even particularly unique to religious people. The culture that invented the Stairmaster and the Nautilus in its worship of the body is hardly a stranger to the idea of embracing physical discomfort for a higher good. All religious traditions have likewise contained at least some element of "disciplining the flesh" in order to free the spirit, and many of these disciplines have been far harsher than anything in the Catholic Tradition.

Certainly the Gnostics—a heretical movement that stressed "salvation by knowledge," and a special focus of praise in *The Da Vinci Code*—had ascetic practices that make Silas' lurid and weird self-abuses seem minor discomforts by comparison. In short, "corporal mortification" is strange only if you think that John the Baptist's prickly shirt of camel hair or Jesus' fasts in the desert are strange. The fact that comfortable Westerners like Brown think this way is more of a comment on comfortable Westerners than it is on the vast majority of the human race who, whether Christian, Buddhist, Native American, Muslim, or Zoroastrian, all have in common the use of physical disciplines for the sake of the good of the soul.

CHAPTER 2

LITTLE LIES PREPARE FOR BIG ONES

8. What is this "secret" Opus Dei organization anyway? Where are its monasteries?

Opus Dei (Latin for "work of God") is not a "secret" organization at all. It is an official Roman Catholic institution founded in 1928 by St. Josemaria Escriva, a Spanish priest. Its purpose is to help ordinary lay people seek holiness in and through their everyday activities, especially through work. Only a small percentage of Opus Dei is clergy; the majority if its members are lay people. There are no monks in Opus Dei, so there is no such thing as an Opus Dei "monastery."

There are a certain few members of Opus Dei known as *numeraries* who choose a vocation of celibacy so they can be totally free to serve the Church. They do not, however, take vows, wear religious clothing of any kind, sleep on straw mats, or spend all their time praying or practicing corporal mortification—in others words, they do not live in the way *The Da Vinci Code* portrays them. They actually work in secular professions.

This fact points out a problem we are going to encounter repeatedly throughout *The Da Vinci Code*: namely, that the author hurls a huge amount of what can only kindly be described as "data" at you. The problem is that he does not tell you which of these "data" are complete fabrications, which are factual but trivial, and which are factual but distorted to support false conclusions. And so, Brown's erroneous view of the Catholic Church ends up creating a character whose life and actions are one of the silliest smears in publishing history. In addition to the inanity of being an albino (!) assassin (now there's somebody who will blend right in and go unnoticed as he carries out his campaign of murder for the subtle masters of intrigue pulling the strings in Rome), poor Silas is saddled with the role of being a "monk" in a Catholic organization that has no monks!

This is the first of many places where Brown doesn't even pass what critic Sandra Miesel, co-author of *The Da Vinci Hoax*, calls the "desk top reference" test. All "impeccable researcher" Brown needed to do was consult an encyclopedia or the Internet to discover that Opus Dei has no monks. But he didn't bother, and he apparently assumed that the reader wouldn't bother, either. This contempt, for both his subject matter and his audience, shows up throughout *The Da Vinci Code*, as we shall see.

9. **Why does Silas kill Saunière, the Louvre curator?**

This, of course, is the mystery that kicks off the story and leads to the big secret about Jesus that the Catholic Church has supposedly been covering up since the very beginning. Rather than get ahead of the story, let's watch it unfold as we move to the hotel where Robert Langdon, the book's hero, is awakened by a phone call.

10. Robert Langdon is a famous symbologist. What is symbology anyway?

Unfortunately, this is not a question we can answer. That's because there *is* no academic discipline known as "symbology." (As such, Harvard University—where Langdon is supposedly a professor—has no department of symbology.) Not that this has stopped reviewers from praising the book by declaring that it will "revolutionize the discipline of symbology." Apparently Brown isn't the only writer who fails Miesel's "desk top reference" test.

In Brown's universe, a symbologist is apparently an academic who goes about delivering the blinding news flash that symbols mean things while frequently remarking on how the little people lack his profound understanding of symbols. For instance, at one point in *The Da Vinci Code*, we are told:

> Langdon was always surprised how few Christians who gazed upon "the crucifix" realized their symbol's violent history was reflected in its very name: "cross" and "crucifix" came from the Latin verb *cruciare*—to torture.

This is a typical example of the air of superiority Brown exudes throughout the book. When read slowly, we discover that this observation means exactly nothing, yet gives the illusion of deeply read erudition. At best, it means "a lot of Christians don't know Latin." True, but so what? The central fact about the crucifix—that it is the symbol of the tortured death of Jesus Christ—is not a mysterious, hidden truth known only to Harvard "symbologists." So what is the point of Langdon's little reflection? Simply this: throughout the book Brown's point is "I'm a great deal smarter than you, and I know the Secret History of Our Times." So he is constantly using Langdon's pseudo-erudition to intimidate the reader into being more susceptible to his "facts" about the "fraudulent origins" of Christianity.

11. I noticed Langdon is described as "Harrison Ford in tweed"? Why is that?

Perhaps Brown was anticipating—or at least hoping—that *The Da Vinci Code* would be made into a movie. Unfortunately, Harrison Ford was apparently unavailable (or uninterested) in playing Langdon, so the role went to Tom Hanks.

12. Sophie Neveu, the book's heroine, seemed kind of promising at first, a strong female character. But then she just spends the rest of the novel saying things like, "What? I had no idea!"

At first glance, Sophie's role is to be Robert Langdon's love interest as per the "standard operating procedure" for thrillers. However, her real role is to be the character the reader identifies with as Brown tutors us in his novel-length seminar on art, history, theology, and the Secret History of the World. Brown offers us a brief, inadequate description of her in which she is praised for her strength and independent intellect. These are, of course, qualities that we as readers would like to think we also have—so we identify with her. Then she promptly drops into the role of wide-eyed student, instructed in the shocking revelations of the supposed "code" by Langdon and Leigh Teabing, the royal British historian and "Grail expert." One of the many ironic hypocrisies of the book is that Langdon, the apostle of "the sacred feminine," doesn't learn anything of any real substance from Sophie, the book's sole major female character. She saves him from the pursuing cops, like a good servant. But her main job in the novel is to sit around and be the amazed female student while two men tell her the "truth" about life, the universe, and everything else. Then, after Langdon—the learned scholar who tells us all about the glories of androgyny—is finished lecturing, her job is to fall into a perfectly ordinary and non-androgynous romantic relationship with him.

CHAPTER 3

BLUNDERS AND LIES ABOUT LEONARDO DAVINCI, HIS ART, AND THE GRAIL MYTH

13. OK. So the book isn't much on characterization. But what about the *ideas* in the book. For instance, who was Da Vinci and what did he know about Jesus?

Here again, we run up against one of the most embarrassing aspects of Dan Brown's baseless claims to be an expert in art and history. Brown routinely refers to the great Renaissance artist, engineer, and scientist as "Da Vinci" and thereby trains millions of readers to do likewise. But the reality is that Leonardo da Vinci has traditionally been known as "Leonardo" for the same reason that Jesus of Nazareth is called "Jesus" and not "of Nazareth" and Francis of Assisi is referred to as "Francis" and not "of Assisi." *Vinci* was Leonardo's home town, not his last name—*da Vinci* simply means "of Vinci." This elementary blunder, enshrined throughout the book (and its very title) is a dead giveaway that, whoever Leonardo is, *The Da Vinci Code* will not be a reliable source of information about him.

The basic facts are as follows. Leonardo da Vinci (1452–1519) was an Italian architect, musician, anatomist, inventor, engineer, sculptor, and painter. In other words, he was the epitome of the "Renaissance man." A towering genius, of prodigious talent and interest in everything in heaven and earth, Leonardo is famous for such paintings as *The Last Supper* and the *Mona Lisa*, as well as for his notebooks (written backwards so they could only be read in a mirror), and for his many inventions and designs, some of which anticipated technological advances that would not be achieved for centuries after his death.

As to what Leonardo knew about Jesus, he certainly knew the same basic facts that every other Italian Catholic of his period knew. For the simple fact is, there is no "code" about Jesus hidden in Leonardo's artwork.

14. **The book asserts that Leonardo da Vinci was a homosexual. I'd never heard that before.**

Yes, Brown asserts that Leonardo was a "flamboyant homosexual." In truth, though, we know virtually nothing of Leonardo's sex life, a fact not very compatible with the claim of flamboyance. There is some very fragmentary evidence that Leonardo may have engaged in homosexual behavior: a charge of sodomy in his youth that was subsequently dismissed. But it is difficult to say for certain since the record simply doesn't address the question. The probable reason Brown makes this claim is because: a) he likes using clichés and "flamboyant homosexual" is a classic cliché; and b) his project demands that Leonardo essentially be a thoroughly modern urbanite running around in Renaissance clothes, with a sophisticated contempt for the Catholic Church.

15. *The Da Vinci Code* **also claims that Leonardo was a "man of reason in an age when science was synonymous with heresy." Was the Church really opposed to science and reason?**

Actually the Church was a generous patron of the sciences and of reason, as is evidenced by the huge number of philosophical giants it produced, e.g., Thomas Aquinas, Anselm, Augustine, and many others. Copernicus, for instance—who Brown claims, in an earlier novel, was murdered by the Church—was a Catholic priest who received no censure whatsoever for his work and died of natural causes. Indeed, as sociologist Rodney Stark has noted, the reason the sciences arose in Europe and gained such ascendancy in ways unparalleled anywhere else in the world is precisely because Christianity, in distinction from virtually every other religious tradition, took reason seriously:

> But, if one digs deeper, it becomes clear that the truly fundamental basis not only for capitalism, but for the rise of the West, was an extraordinary faith in *reason*.

> A series of developments, in which reason won the day, gave unique shape to Western culture and institutions. And the most important of those victories occurred within Christianity. While the other world religions emphasized mystery and intuition, Christianity alone embraced reason and logic as the primary guides to religious truth.

... from early days, the church fathers taught that reason was the supreme gift from God and the means to progressively increase understanding of Scripture and revelation. Consequently Christianity was oriented to the future, while the other major religions asserted the superiority of the past. Encouraged by the scholastics and embodied in the great medieval universities founded by the church, faith in the power of reason infused Western culture, stimulating the pursuit of science and the evolution of democratic theory and practice.

During the past century Western intellectuals have been more than willing to trace European imperialism to Christian origins, but they have been entirely unwilling to recognize that Christianity made any contribution (other than intolerance) to the Western capacity to dominate other societies. Rather, the West is said to have surged ahead precisely as it overcame religious barriers to progress, especially those impeding science. Nonsense. The success of the West, including the rise of science, rested entirely on religious foundations, and the people who brought it about were devout Christians. (*Source:* Rodney Stark, "How Christianity [and Capitalism] Led to Science," *The Chronicle of Higher Education*, December 2, 2005)

Brown, however, finds historical facts inconvenient to his project of portraying the Renaissance Church as a despotic power terrified of knowledge. This lands him in a humorous self-contradiction as he simultaneously claims that Leonardo, the man of reason and science, was allegedly living in fear of the Vatican's superstitious hatred of scientists such as himself while simultaneously receiving "hundreds" of "lucrative Vatican commissions." The crowning irony here is that Leonardo, in fact, received *one* commission from the Vatican in his entire life—and was never accused of any sort of heresy. But since this does not fit in with the image of a clever sophisticate who got away with subverting the dim-witted (yet ruthlessly ingenious) Catholic Church by painting "subversive" art right under its very nose, Brown simply ignores the facts and delivers yet another falsehood.

We are also told by Brown that Leonardo was a "worshiper of Nature's divine order," yet a "spiritual hypocrite" who, for the money, created an "enormous" amount of Christian art riddled with codes attacking the Christian faith. This, being translated, is a claim that Leonardo was really a pagan worshiper of the "sacred feminine" who adored Nature rather than the God who made Nature. However, Brown alleges, since it was too dangerous for a sophisticated man like Leonardo to do this openly, he got the word out via secret code right under the noses of his ignorant Catholic patrons through his "enormous" output of artwork.

The main problem is that there is absolutely no evidence for this incredible claim and plenty of evidence against it. For instance, it just isn't so that Leonardo's artistic output is "enormous." Leonardo left us a legacy of seventeen paintings, four of which are unfinished. That's it. And of these, the most famous of all, the *Mona Lisa*, is not a "Christian" work at all, but a portrait of a merchant's wife.

16. **Yes, but Langdon says the *Mona Lisa* is really religious, being an anagram of the pagan god *Amon* and his consort *Isis*.**

Sorry, but no. This is yet another indication of Brown's failure to even check an encyclopedia or the Internet before making such an embarrassingly ignorant claim. For Leonardo da Vinci never called the painting the *Mona Lisa*. He called it *La Gioconda*. The title *Mona Lisa* comes from Giorgio Vasari's biography of Leonardo da Vinci, published thirty-one years after his death. In this work, Vasari identifies the woman in the painting as Lisa, the wife of wealthy Florentine businessman Francesco del Giocondo. (*Mona* is a common Italian contraction of *madonna* meaning "my lady," so the title literally means "My Lady Lisa.") The name *Mona Lisa* was not commonly used to refer to the painting until long after Leonardo's death. Likewise, the rest of Langdon's "analysis" is simply hogwash. No reputable art scholar believes that the *Mona Lisa* is really a self-portrait of Leonardo in drag or a coded message about the glories of androgyny.

The simple fact is Brown, who has no qualifications in art history, is just making this stuff up. So we should take his claim that "all descriptions of artwork ... are accurate" with a very large grain of salt. To be accurate, one should, at minimum, know who a portrait portrays and what its actual name is before you start making confident declarations about what it means—especially when you are going to use your declarations to make inflammatory claims about the fraudulent origins of Christianity.

17. What's the deal with *The Vitruvian Man*?

In the book, clue number one to the trail of puzzles that Langdon must follow to find out the "Big Secret" is the way in which Saunière arranges his body as he is dying: spread eagle and naked, with a pentacle drawn on his stomach from his own blood. The basic purpose in the story is to point to the next big clue: that everything is all about Leonardo da Vinci. This particular image is supposed to do that because Saunière, it turns out, is trying to refer Langdon to *The Vitruvian Man*. This is one of the most famous of Leonardo's illustrations, showing a naked human figure spread eagle in a circle with his arms and legs in two different positions. Brown ties *The Vitruvian Man* to the symbol of the pentacle and then proceeds from there to quickly link it all, with sweeping claims, to the history of the "sacred feminine" in paganism and to charges that the Church somehow managed to transform pentacles (which allegedly represent the feminine) into satanic symbols as part of a "Vatican campaign." The evidence for this is exactly zero, but it sets up the argument throughout the book that the Church allegedly hates the feminine (which would certainly be news to the Blessed Virgin Mary) and that Leonardo was the bearer of the alleged Great Secret of Jesus' marriage to Mary Magdalene, the "true holy Grail," and of the fraudulent origins of the Church.

18. What is the Grail myth?

The Grail myth generally holds that St. Joseph of Arimathea (who, in the third chapter of John's gospel, visited Jesus and in whose tomb Christ was buried) took the cup that Christ used at the Last Supper and caught some of His blood with it as He hung from the Cross. The Grail was held to have various miraculous/magical powers. In most English versions of the legend, St. Joseph eventually took the Grail to England and hid it. It is this Grail that King Arthur and his Knights of the Round Table seek in the Arthurian legend.

In contrast to this is the assertion of *The Da Vinci Code* that the "true" Grail was not a cup, but Mary Magdalene, who allegedly bore the "blood of Christ" in the form of a child who went on to found a line of French kings.

19.   What about the strange pun on *San Greal* (Holy Grail) and *Sang Real* (Royal Blood)? Doesn't that suggest there's something to Brown's thesis?

No. Actually, the French for "royal blood" is *sang royal*, so the pun is non-existent. In addition, the legend of the Grail is, in fact, a deeply Catholic one, since it centers on the Eucharist and makes very clear the link between the blood shed by Christ on the Cross and the blood of Christ offered to the world in the Holy Sacrifice of the Mass. In short, every Eucharistic cup is a Grail, and the royal blood each contains is the blood of Jesus, the King of Kings. The Catholic claim is, if anything, far more shocking than just another tale of a humdrum romantic tryst. For, in baptism, Christ teaches that we become members of His Royal Family, with Christ Himself, the Son of King David, as our elder brother and God as our Father.

20. **But what about all the strange clues in Leonardo da Vinci's painting *The Last Supper*? Isn't the figure sitting on Jesus' right actually a woman?**

No. That's St. John the Evangelist, the "beloved disciple," not Mary Magdalene.

21. **If that's so, then why does he look so feminine?**

Because that was an enormously popular way of portraying youth in the Renaissance. The key to understanding *The Last Supper* is not by looking for dubious "codes" but by comparing it to the rest of Leonardo's work and to the norms of Renaissance painting in general. When you do, you will discover that male youths are frequently portrayed with feminine faces and masculine bodies. John, traditionally the youngest of the apostles, is frequently portrayed as a beardless youth and hence with just those feminine qualities so common in Renaissance art. The painting reveals not that Mary Magdalene has crashed the Last Supper, but the moment at which Jesus has declared "one of you will betray me." That's why all the apostles look shocked and are talking excitedly to each other. As the gospel of John makes clear, John was seated closest to Jesus and so Peter asked John to ask Jesus who He meant (John 13:21-25). That is what the painting depicts—i.e., Peter leaning close to John to whisper the question. The reason John is seated at Jesus' right is that he is, as the Bible describes him, the "beloved disciple," and is therefore seated in the traditional place of honor to the right of the host. It's a painting that is perfectly congruent with traditional Catholic and biblical teaching. No "codes" are required to understand it.

22. **What about the fact that the "V" shape representing the female womb and the Grail is at the focal point of *The Last Supper*? Doesn't this suggest that's what Leonardo is really trying to get us to see?**

It might—if, in fact, a "V" shape representing the female womb and the Grail were at the focal point of *The Last Supper*. However, once again Brown fails the encyclopedia test. A quick look at *The Last Supper* either in a book or online quickly shows that its focal point is the head of Jesus, not a "V" shape. Brown is again crossing his fingers and hoping you will feel cowed enough by his phony erudition that you will simply take his word for it and not go look for yourself.

23. **But if Mary Magdalene is not the true Grail, then why does Leonardo paint Jesus without a cup at the Last Supper?**

For some reason, people will more readily believe a really huge lie than a small one. Brown bears out this principle with the central artistic claim of *The Da Vinci Code*: that the figure seated to Jesus' right is Mary Magdalene and that Leonardo da Vinci deliberately portrays Jesus without a cup in front of Him in order to reveal the hidden truth that Mary Magdalene is the true holy Grail, the vessel containing the "blood" of Jesus in the form of a child. It's a claim of such huge implications that literally millions of readers never think to do the obvious thing: go back and take a careful look at the painting of *The Last Supper* and count the cups on the table. When we do, we find that there *are* thirteen cups corresponding to Jesus and the twelve disciples. So there is no missing cup. It's right there on the table along with the twelve cups of the twelve apostles.

CHAPTER 4

BLUNDERS AND LIES ABOUT THE PRIORY OF SION AND THE KNIGHTS TEMPLAR

24. **But wasn't Leonardo one of the "grand masters" of the Priory of Sion and privy to some great secret? The "FACT" page at the beginning of the book says that the *Bibliothèque Nationale* proves that Leonardo was a member, along with a lot of other famous people.**

Brown's claims for the supposed secrets hidden in Leonardo's artwork (again, claims made by someone with no training in art, archaeology, history, or theology) rest on the premise that Leonardo was a member of a secret organization called the Priory of Sion. According to Brown, the Knights Templar, a military order that conquered Jerusalem during the First Crusade, set up a secret group known as the Priory of Sion in 1099. The Priory then supposedly excavated the Temple Mount —the hill upon which the Temple of Jerusalem had stood until its destruction by the Romans in A.D. 70—and stumbled on an ancient record revealing the shocking truth that Jesus had married Mary Magdalene. After His death (in Brown's world, there is no Resurrection), she bore His child and went to France, where the bloodline she founded eventually became a line of French kings called the Merovingians.

Brown gives a veneer of credibility to these claims on his FACT page. He tells us that the Priory of Sion was founded in 1099. True. What he *doesn't* tell us is that the last members of the Priory joined the Jesuits in 1617 and the Priory ceased to exist at that point. This would have made it awfully difficult for Sir Isaac Newton or Victor Hugo to be members and it casts considerable doubt on whether Leonardo could have been a member either.

This doubt only deepens when we discover that the sole documentation for this claim depends on the writings of one Pierre Plantard, a French anti-Semitic crank who founded a *new* Priory of Sion in 1956. Plantard then wrote lots of *National Enquirer*-quality articles claiming to link his secret society to the medieval Priory. In the 1960s and 70s, some of this unsubstantiated nonsense was repeated as fact by authors of other crank books such as *The Templar Revelation* and *Holy Blood, Holy Grail* (more on these later). Brown simply accepts their claims with complete credulity—and passes it on to the reader as "FACT."

25. But what about the secret parchments that identify the past "grand masters" of the Priory of Sion?

One of the most damning of Brown's "factual" assertions is his claim that the mysterious parchments known as *Les Dossieres Secrets*, supposedly identifying past "grand masters" of the Priory, were found in Paris' *Bibliothèque Nationale* in 1975. The problem is that not even the authors of *The Templar Revelation* regard these documents as genuine, largely because investigators discovered they were printed on the same press used by Plantard to print his right-wing newsletters and broadsides.

In short, there was a real Priory of Sion founded in 1099, but it has no relationship to the Priory of Sion that exists today. There is no reputable evidence that Leonardo da Vinci even heard of the original Priory, much less was a member. Nor did the original Priory have any "grand masters" for the simple reason that the head of a *priory* is called a *prior*, not a *grand master*.

26. So there's no evidence supporting Brown's claims about Leonardo da Vinci's connection to the Priory of Sion. Still, I'm intrigued. What exactly was the Priory of Sion?

In 1099, Western European Crusaders, after liberating the Holy Land from Muslim control, built a new church in Jerusalem on the ruins of an ancient Byzantine church called *Hagia Sion* (Holy Zion). The new church was named St. Mary's, and a group of priests who served there were known as the *Prieuré de Notre Dame de Sion* (the Priory of Our Lady of Sion), neatly combining the names of both churches. They remained there until 1217 when St. Mary's was destroyed by the Islamic re-conquest of Jerusalem. At that point, they withdrew to Sicily to continue their ministry. The Priory struggled on for four more centuries until its last members joined the Jesuits in 1617. In short, the Priory of Sion was one of many orders and societies that have come and gone over the long history of the Catholic Church.

27. **In *The Da Vinci Code*, Brown indicates that the secret knowledge of the Priory regarding the marriage of Jesus and Mary Magdalene made it possible for the Knights Templar to blackmail the Catholic Church?   Is this true?**

The real question is, "What evidence is offered in *The Da Vinci Code* to back up such an outrageous claim?" Actually, the book offers no evidence at all because there is none. Indeed, there is no evidence whatsoever that the original Priory of Sion was: a) related in any way to the Knights Templar; b) involved in any excavations on the Temple Mount; c) connected with any documentation of a marriage between Jesus and Mary Magdalene; d) connected with Leonardo da Vinci; or e) connected in any way with the "Priory of Sion" founded in 1956 by Pierre Plantard.

Therefore, there is no evidence at all that the Priory of Sion or the Knights Templar had any sensational information about the relationship between Jesus and Mary Magdalene with which to blackmail the Church.

28. **So who were the Knights Templar and how did they become so powerful?**

The Knights Templar was the largest and most powerful of the military orders that arose during the Crusades. They were founded in 1118 for the purpose of helping the newly re-conquered Holy Land maintain its defenses against the Muslim forces that sought to retake it. They became powerful not by digging up the secret of Jesus' marriage and by blackmailing the Church with it, but by being heavily involved in the entire political and financial infrastructure of the re-conquered Holy Land and, in time, with much of Europe as well.

29. So, at the very least, they were involved in the evil Crusades.

The idea that the Crusades were essentially evil is another example of historical revisionism, of looking at the past with a contemporary lens. In fact, the Crusades (of which there were eight, the first beginning in the year 1096 and the last in 1270) were enormously complex affairs. Their basic goal was to defend eastern Christians from the onslaught of Muslims who had conquered the Holy Land, North Africa, Spain, and much of the Middle East, and who were continuing to conquer more and more of what had once been Christian lands. Eastern Christians asked their European brethren to help defend them, and they went. The only truly successful Crusade was the first, in which the Holy Land was re-conquered and Jerusalem was won back from the Muslims in 1099. A century later, however, Jerusalem was lost again and the Holy Land once again became an Islamic dominion. No subsequent Crusade was a success, with the possible exception of the *reconquista* (strictly speaking, not considered one of the Crusades), which succeeded in driving the Moors out of Spain in the 15th century. After the period of the Crusades, Islam continued its expansion by *jihad* (i.e., holy war) until its territorial growth via conquest was halted by

Christian victories in the famous battles of Lepanto in 1571 and Vienna in 1683.

30. Did the Catholic Church really wipe out the Knights Templar in a single night?

One of the more outrageous slanders in *The Da Vinci Code* is the claim that "the Vatican" (which did not even exist at this point in history), in order to silence the Templars and end their blackmailing threats to reveal the "truth" about Jesus, engineered a vast plot spanning all of Europe to annihilate the Templars in a single night. Like all good lies, this one contains just enough truth to be convincing yet is a gross distortion of history.

While it is true that the Templars were cruelly persecuted and ultimately suppressed, the problem is that it was Philip IV ("Philip the Fair"), king of France and bitter enemy of the Pope, who did the persecuting and suppressing. Contrary to Brown's lurid claims, the fact is that Philip went to the Templars seeking financing for one of his wars. The Templars refused, so Philip demanded that Pope Boniface VIII excommunicate them. The Pope refused, so Philip sent mercenaries to Rome to assault and kidnap him. Boniface died as a consequence of this rough treatment. His successor, Benedict XI, lifted the excommunication of Philip that had resulted from his attack on Boniface but refused to exonerate the king's agent who had engineered the attack. Benedict then died suddenly (it is strongly suspected that Philip's agent poisoned him) and was succeeded by Clement V, who moved the papacy to Avignon,

France. Clement reluctantly gave in to Philip's demands. The papal investigations of both the Knights Templar as a whole and of its individual members found almost no knights guilty of heresy outside of France. Meanwhile, the fifty-four knights executed in France were killed because King Philip—not the Pope—wanted them dead. In short, "the Vatican" was: a) not at the Vatican (or anywhere in Rome, for that matter) but at Avignon; b) was at most a reluctant and powerless tool of the French king ; and c) had nothing to do with some vast pan-European conspiracy against the Templars. The driving force here was not some plot by the Catholic Church to stop a centuries-old blackmail plot concerning Jesus' marriage. Rather, it was the desire of Philip to remove an obstacle to his dreams of power.

31. Why does Brown fill *The Da Vinci Code* with so much "junk" history and art analysis when it's easy to find out it is inaccurate ?

Laura Miller, a critic for the decidedly non-Christian online magazine *Salon*, offers one reasonable possibility in her essay "The Da Vinci Crock":

> You get the impression Brown never expected *The Da Vinci Code* to take the world by storm or that it would invite the kind of scrutiny his novel cannot withstand. As a result, Brown makes several dumb, careless mistakes that put the lie to his pretensions of extensive research, such as having a "Grail expert" describe the Dead Sea Scrolls as being "among the earliest Christian records," when the documents are Jewish and do not mention Jesus Christ at all. (*Source*:

www.salon.com/books/feature/2004/12/29/
da_vinci_code/index1.html)

In short, the basic reason the book gets so much wrong is that Brown probably didn't expect it to become such a cultural phenomenon and therefore assumed nobody would bother to check his claims. Now that it has become a mega-bestseller, he is stuck with having to defend his shoddy research. His defense is twofold: First, he states repeatedly that "It's only a story" so that critics are made to look ridiculous for complaining about errors in a work of fiction. Second, he constantly plays up the "impeccable research" angle, always insisting on the historical accuracy of his claims. (Notice the logical contradiction in these two aspects of Brown's defense.) The average reader is overwhelmed by this approach, and the informed critic is made to look like a nitpicking curmudgeon.

Chapter 5

Brown's Sources

32. Where does Brown get his information?

Much of it he seems to have made up. The rest he apparently took from others who just made it up. Brown gets the bulk of his information from just a few books—all of them regarded as laughably inaccurate by serious scholars. His primary source is *Holy Blood, Holy Grail* by Michael Baigent, Richard Leigh, and Henry Lincoln. Brown either pays homage to these men or insults them as he plagiarizes them (depending on your viewpoint) by naming his duplicitous character Leigh Teabing ("Leigh" being taken from "Richard Leigh" and "Teabing" being an anagram of "Baigent").

33. What's *Holy Blood, Holy Grail* about?

This controversial book, published in 1982, basically makes the same claims as *The Da Vinci Code*: that Jesus married Mary Magdalene and she bore His child, eventually leading to the establishment of the Merovingian dynasty in France, which in turn gave rise to the Grail legend. Brown's only real contribution is to place these historically ludicrous claims within the context of a rudimentary mystery, with a series of "puzzles" to solve, escapes from the cops to pull off, and the vague suggestion of romance near the end between Langdon and Sophie.

34. What kind of research supports the claims of *Holy Blood, Holy Grail?*

Again, *Salon*'s Laura Miller answers this question pretty succinctly when she writes of authors Baigent, Leigh, and Lincoln:

> When it comes to spinning a masterful line of bull, they have few equals, and if we cannot admire them, we can at least respect their peculiar genius, much as Sherlock Holmes respected the Napoleon of crime, Professor Moriarty.
>
> Baigent, Leigh, and Lincoln are the Moriartys of pseudohistory, and *Holy Blood, Holy Grail* is their great triumph. Their techniques include burying their readers in chin-high drifts of factoids—some valid but irrelevant, some uncheckable (the untranslated diaries of obscure 17th-century clerics, and so on), others, like the labyrinthine family trees of various medieval French noblemen, simply numbing, and if you trouble to figure them out, pretty inconclusive. A preposterous idea will first be floated as a guess (it is "not inconceivable" that the Knights Templar found documentation of Jesus and Mary Magdalene's marriage in Jerusalem), then later presented as a tentative hypothesis, then still later treated as a fact that must be accounted for (the knights had to take those documents somewhere, so it must have been the south of France!).
>
> Each detail requires extensive effort to track down and verify, but anyone who succeeds

in proving it false comes across as a mere nitpicker—and still has a blizzard of other pseudo facts to contend with. The miasma of bogus authenticity that the authors of *Holy Blood, Holy Grail* create becomes impenetrable; you might as well use a rifle to fight off a thick fog.

Nevertheless, the Grail theory touted in *Holy Blood, Holy Grail* and *The Da Vinci Code* can be broken down into two main parts: One concerns the historical details of Jesus' life and the establishment of orthodox Christian tenets in the three centuries after His death. The second part describes the survival of the suppressed, hidden and unorthodox "truth" about Jesus and His descendants via the Priory of Sion and its military arm, the Knights Templar. Clues to this truth are supposedly embedded in the art, architecture and literature produced by the intellectual superstars who, with the occasional aristocrat, are said to have run the Priory of Sion. Why people who are sworn to keep this secret would go around planting all these clues is never explained. (*Source*: www.salon.com/books/feature/2004/12/29/da_vinci_code/index1.html)

35. I heard the authors of *Holy Blood, Holy Grail* are suing Dan Brown. Is that true?

Yes. As of this writing, the authors of *Holy Blood, Holy Grail* are suing Dan Brown for plagiarism. They claim, with much evidence in their favor, that Brown's "impeccably researched" book includes a number of long passages which essentially reproduce their own text without attribution.

36. Are there any other sources behind *The Da Vinci Code* besides *Holy Blood, Holy Grail*?

Yes. Several other books of similarly dubious credentials are part of Brown's "impeccable research." One of these is *The Woman with the Alabaster Jar* by Margaret Starbird, who read *Holy Blood, Holy Grail* and found in it the excuse to abandon common sense and accurate history. Starbird posits a number of totally unfounded theories about Mary Magdalene as a kind of proto-feminist advocate of goddess worship. The historical basis for this silly idea, as we shall see, is simply nonexistent; it is rooted in wishful thinking on the part of modern neo-pagan feminists and the desire to invent a new religion (with a new, and bogus, history to support it).

In addition, Brown uses *The Templar Revelation*, a 1998 book by Lynn Picknett and Clive Prince, which also makes much of Mary Magdalene's supposed role in the early Church as a rival to the apostles. The ironic and amusing thing about *The Templar Revelation* is that it forms a core part of Brown's argument *even though it contradicts both Brown and itself on two crucial points!*

First, and most importantly, *The Templar Revelation* argues for women's ordination to the priesthood on the grounds that Mary Magdalene was the first witness of Christ's resurrection. Amazingly, though, the authors then go on to deny that the resurrection ever took place! By doing so, they undercut their very argument for Mary Magdalene's alleged priesthood, since the whole point of the priesthood is to offer the sacrifice of the Mass in memory of Christ's death and resurrection.

Second, *The Templar Revelation* dismisses one of the first things Brown alleges as "FACT" by refuting the validity of *Les Dossieres Secrets*. In doing so, its authors destroy the basis of Brown's claim that Leonardo was a "grand master" of the Priory of Sion and heir to the "great secret" it supposedly guarded concerning Jesus and Mary Magdalene.

37. **OK. So what do we have so far when it comes to Brown's claims versus actual fact?**

Basically nothing. *The Da Vinci Code* begins with "FACT" claims that, as we have seen, are not factual (and that are even contradicted by Brown's own sources). From there the book moves on to demonstrably false and slanderous claims about Opus Dei, nonsense about "missing cups" in Leonardo's *The Last Supper* that can be refuted by simply looking at the painting, artistically illiterate claims about the supposed "woman" seated next to Jesus in *The Last Supper*, historically illiterate anagrams about the *Mona Lisa*, linguistically illiterate claims about the Grail, and erroneous nonsense about the history of the Priory of Sion that even *The Templar Revelation* rejects. In short, we find there is absolutely no basis for a claim that the Priory (or any other "secret society," for that matter) ever had any evidence of Jesus' marriage to Mary Magdalene, much less that this secret society included Leonardo da Vinci as its "grand master."

CHAPTER 6

THE FIRST GOAL OF *THE DA VINCI CODE*: THE DESTRUCTION OF THE GOSPEL

38. Sometimes Langdon says that all these incredible secrets have been known for centuries by scholars, but at other times he insists that this "secret knowledge" has been cleverly covered up by the Church and nobody knows about it. How can both claims be true?

Logically, they cannot. But remember, *The Da Vinci Code* doesn't have a burning interest in truth. If we read its claims not as attempts to tell truth, but as attempts to manipulate us into believing a lie, we can then understand the motivation for its many contradictions. Brown's strategy is to intimidate the reader with his phony erudition. Then, he inflames the reader's pride at discovering a blockbuster secret about Jesus and Christianity.

To intimidate, few things work as well as making the reader feel ignorant. And so, we see Langdon and Teabing continually delivering lectures to a wide-eyed Sophie, who (like the reader) exclaims, "What? I had no idea!" as each alleged "revelation" is unfolded. They then pat her (and us) on the head and refer to her as "dear girl" while constantly reiterating the mantra that "scholars have known all this for ages." Since most readers don't know much about Leonardo da Vinci, the Priory of Sion, Aramaic, Greek, the Council of Nicea, or the way in which the Bible was written and assembled by the Church, they feel stupid. People of faith may feel embarrassed because whatever they say to articulate their beliefs sounds like the protests of a child who has just been shown the Santa suit in the closet and informed that "it's all a lie."

We can see this at the heart of the novel when Teabing bluntly declares that "Many scholars claim that the early Church literally stole Jesus from His original followers." In his patronizing way, Teabing makes clear Brown's message: "What I mean," he says, "is that almost everything our fathers taught us about Christ is *false*."

Nobody likes to feel stupid, of course. And nobody likes the feeling of being a sucker. Brown plays on these aversions with the second part of his strategy. Having persuaded you that the Christian herd is just a bunch of suckers, he offers you the chance to escape suckerdom by buying into his newly revealed "truth." If you accept his claims that "scholars have known this for ages," he promises you liberation from the mental slavery you have lived in all your life. It's an appealing sophistry and many people fall for it. Yet, in doing so, they are actually falling prey to the manipulation they think they are escaping.

39. **Teabing, Langdon's scholar friend, turns out to be a bad guy. Couldn't that be Brown's way of saying this harsh assessment of Christianity is wrong?**

It would be nice if that were the case. But the reality is that Teabing's assertions about the false origins of Christianity are endorsed by the "good guy" Langdon. Brown seems to be using the standard "good cop/bad cop" mode of persuasion to get the reader to swallow his argument. Langdon isn't as nasty, cynical, and villainous as Teabing, so he comes off sounding like the voice of reason. Teabing, because of his duplicity, is denied the chance to reach the object of the Grail quest. But at the end of the novel, everything asserted by Teabing turns out to be "true," and Langdon (the "worthy servant of the Grail") is found pretty much worshiping the bones of Mary Magdalene, the "outcast sacred feminine" and spouse of the mere mortal prophet, Jesus. So Brown manipulates the reader into embracing Teabing's claims about the origins of Christianity. Sophie, it turns out, is a descendant of Jesus, the Gospel is a fraud, the Church is a vast Murder Incorporated organization, and you, the reader, are now one of the chosen few who see, along with Sophie and Langdon, the blinding truth of the glory of the "sacred feminine" and the promise of a return to pagan worship.

40. Why does Brown make all these shocking claims about Leonardo, the Priory of Sion, and Mary Magdalene if they're not true?

Partly, of course, because they form the set up for the central, "shocking revelation" of the novel: that Jesus intended for us to worship the "sacred feminine" rather than the God of Israel, incarnate in His person. But this, of course, leads to the deeper point: Why does Brown set *that* up as his "shocking revelation"? The answer is that he is attempting to create a new religious myth in which the Christian faith in general and the Catholic faith in particular is definitively refuted and replaced by a "sacred feminine" form of paganism.

41. But isn't the essential thing about a religion its timeless truths rather than its historical claims?

Not always. If a religion is founded on some universal moral principle such as "Abandon the desires of the flesh," it does not require roots in history. Thus, Buddhism would not be harmed if it could be proven that Buddha (i.e, Siddhartha Gautama) never existed. Why? Because the point of Buddhism is not Buddha himself but the *teachings* of Buddha. But religions that are essentially rooted in history—such as Judaism or Christianity—*do* stand or fall on the validity of their historical claims, because they are about *persons*, not merely ideas.

Judaism, for instance, exists because it is rooted in an historical claim: that the One God of the Universe entered into a covenant with the Jewish people through the ministry of Moses. If that claim can be shown to be false, then Judaism itself is false. Imagine if somebody wrote a book about the "real" Moses and the "secret origins" of Judaism, claiming that the entire Jewish religion is based on a pack of lies. What if it said the "historical" Moses was really a Hindu-like mystic who believed in many deities and preached tolerance and free love? He did not lead the people out of Egypt in the Exodus, did not give the Ten Commandments, performed no miracles, and gave no moral rules.

Suppose this same book claimed that, centuries later, the Jewish priests who claimed to be Moses' successors rewrote their nation's history and decided to give Moses an "upgrade." They turned him into a prophet who saw the one true God and spoke with Him. They then made him into a great military leader who defeated Pharaoh and led his people out of slavery. In effect, the Jewish priests created Moses in their own image—a priest like themselves—leading the people in worship and animal sacrifice. And they recast Moses as a divinely appointed moral teacher who gave the people Ten Commandments from God Himself on Mount Sinai, thus establishing the covenant with God.

Then, imagine that the book argued that the Jewish priests did all this to strengthen their own positions of power. For the priests wanted to be recognized as the divinely appointed leaders of the people, the teachers of a God-given law, and the spokesmen for God—just like the Moses they invented. So in the end, many core Jewish beliefs are really based on lies told by these power-hungry priests who successfully duped the people in their efforts to solidify their political control over Israel. And many Jews have fallen for the "legend of Moses" ever since.

Such a book would be widely condemned as being anti-Semitic and a direct assault on Judaism—and rightly so. But when Dan Brown comes out with an anti-Catholic conspiracy theory novel, we are assured that "It's just a story!" As Philip Jenkins, distinguished professor of history and religious studies at Pennsylvania State University, has recently argued, anti-Catholicism is the last acceptable

American prejudice (see Phillip Jenkins, *The New Anti-Catholicism: The Last Acceptable Prejudice*, Oxford University Press, 2003). The phenomenal success of a book like *The Da Vinci Code* bears this out.

42. But can't we affirm the core teachings of Christianity without believing that Jesus is the divine "Son of God"?

No. The whole point of Christianity is the person of Jesus. *He* is the core teaching. Jesus' teaching about morality, His miracles, and virtually everything recorded in the gospels only make sense in light of the core teaching about who He is and what He accomplished by dying and rising from the dead. If we were to take that away, we would not end up with "the true essence of Jesus' teaching." We would end up with nothing because who Jesus *is* forms the absolute heart of the Gospel. That's why the gospels more or less glide over the details of Jesus' earthly life and devote roughly a quarter of their ink to a 72-hour period in the life of their subject—His passion, death, and resurrection. Trying to make the gospels about Jesus and His girlfriend—as Brown seeks to do in *The Da Vinci Code*—is like reading the story of Martin Luther King, Jr., and pretending that the main point of his life was not the civil rights' struggle but just an interest in chatting about moral philosophy as he took long strolls with a few friends through Selma, Alabama. Ignoring the reasons for Jesus' death— namely, His claims to be the divine Son of God—is like saying that Dr. King died suddenly in Memphis without mentioning that he was murdered for what he preached.

Bottom line: Jesus did not come to give us timeless abstract truths and moral advice. Rather, He claimed to be God Incarnate, sent to take away the sins of the world. If Jesus is not God and His passion and resurrection did not occur, then, as Teabing says, Christianity is simply false.

43. But if *The Da Vinci Code* is fundamentally anti-Catholic, why do some Catholics in the book receive a favorable portrayal? What about the nun at the Church of St. Sulpice who gets murdered by Silas?

The key to reading *The Da Vinci Code* is that the only "good" Catholic is a bad (i.e., unbelieving) Catholic. That is, a Catholic who dissents from the teachings of the Catholic Church. So the various Catholic figures (e.g., Brown's version of Leonardo da Vinci) who are laboring to undermine the faith of the Catholic Church are the "good guys." Likewise, the nun who exudes resentment at Catholic teaching is good. But, of course, every character who is portrayed as a believing orthodox Catholic is portrayed as deceptive (Fache), murderous and psychopathic (Silas), obese and corrupt (Vatican officials), ignorant and afraid of science (Bishop Aringarosa), and so forth.

44. So, according to *The Da Vinci Code*, good Catholics are those who oppose the Gospel of Jesus Christ?

Yes. *The Da Vinci Code*'s point is not that Catholics have sinned by failing to live up to their principles. Rather, the book's central claim is that the essential principles and teachings of the Catholic faith (and indeed of the Bible itself) are a *complete and total fraud* from beginning to end. *The Da Vinci Code* aims at nothing less than the rejection of the worship of Jesus Christ as the crucified and risen Son of God and the creation of a new myth that legitimates a return to the pagan worship of gods and goddesses.

CHAPTER 7

THE SECOND GOAL OF *THE DA VINCI CODE*: THE GLORIFICATION OF PAGANISM

45. *The Da Vinci Code* **claims that all pagans celebrated the "sacred feminine" and that the Catholic Church stamped this out. Is that right?**

Yes, that's exactly what *The Da Vinci Code* claims. Brown, discussing this issue in a television interview, explains that, "In the early days . . . we lived in a world of gods and goddesses . . . Every Mars had an Athena. The god of war had the goddess of beauty; in the Egyptian tradition, Osiris and Isis . . . And now we live in a world solely of gods. The female counterpart has been erased" (CNN, July 17, 2003).

But, in fact, although goddess worship was prevalent in the ancient world, it was not universal. Some pagans worshiped goddesses; some worshiped no gods at all and regarded belief in gods as ignorant superstition; some worshiped one God; some honored a huge pantheon of gods. Some made no distinction between earthly creatures and gods, while others clearly understood that earthly creatures where merely representations of spiritual realities. Some pagans were philosophers who looked at gods as abstractions, while others practiced mystery cults devoted solely to masculine deities, feminine deities, or animal totems. Some believed in magic, others in science, and many in both. In short, "all" pagans had only one thing in common: they were not Christians or Jews. The notion that worship of the "sacred feminine" was universally practiced throughout pre-Christian paganism is simply false.

46. So what *is* paganism anyway?

Paganism is essentially the worship of *creatures* instead of the Creator. The choice to worship creatures can be made in ignorance or deliberately. Pre-Christian paganism typically worshiped creatures in ignorance. Paul described such pagans as "feeling after" God in the book of Acts, chapter 17, i.e., they were seeking—but did not know how to find—the one true God. Post-Christian paganism, such as *The Da Vinci Code* advocates, consciously rejects the one God in order to worship creatures. Peter Kreeft describes the difference between pre- and post-Christian paganism as the difference between a virgin and a divorcee. Pre-Christian paganism was seeking God, although in error; post-Christian paganism is seeking a substitute for God.

Once the choice is made to worship creatures, history has shown that virtually any creature—from a dung beetle to a human being—can and will be worshiped. As the old saying goes, when people don't believe in God, they don't believe in nothing—they believe in anything.

47. So what's the big deal about the "sacred feminine"?

In *The Da Vinci Code*, Brown basically argues that Christianity has stamped out the "sacred feminine" and replaced the "true goddess" with an all-male God. His proposed solution: re-introduce goddess worship! The book claims that this is what Jesus intended to do by exalting Mary Magdalene and entrusting the Church to her, not Peter. However, according to Brown, instead of the Church being handed over to her, the evil apostles—whom Jesus inexplicably chose to follow Him, despite their obvious sexist tendencies—instead took over the Church after Jesus' death, suppressed the role of Mary Magdalene, and established an all-male hierarchy under the leadership of Peter. Then, when Constantine came along three centuries later, he elevated Jesus to divine status in order to make the Church more powerful and use it as an instrument for controlling his subjects.

48. What is the rite of *Hieros Gamos* all about?

In *The Da Vinci Code*, Sophie relates how she once walked in on her grandfather, Saunière, engaging in a ritual sex act. As the story unfolds, we're told that this was the *Hieros Gamos*, a religious ritual by which man and woman are made whole in the reuniting of the "sacred masculine" and "sacred feminine." According to Langdon, Christianity "banished the sacred feminine from the temples of the world," but Saunière kept the "true flame" alive by preserving this rite in memory of the marriage between Jesus (i.e., the "sacred masculine") and Mary Magdalene (the "sacred feminine"). Poor Sophie is just unenlightened; she needs to recognize that her grandfather was really a deeply spiritual man and that the evil Catholic Church (which murdered him) is bent on stamping out all connection between the feminine and the divine.

There are several problems with this bit of psychological manipulation. First, the "rite of *Heiros Gamos*" is bogus, an invention of Margaret Starbird, one of Brown's "scholarly sources." Second, Brown contradicts himself by insisting that nobody thought Jesus (much less Mary Magdalene) was divine until A.D. 325. If this is so, then what is Jesus doing acting as the "sacred masculine"? Third, the notion that the feminine has been banished from the Catholic Church is simply nonsense given the immense role that the Blessed Virgin Mary plays in Catholic belief and practice. And finally, the assertion that only paganism has a place for "sacred sex" is simply false. Christian marriage, after all, is the sacramental union of a man and woman that is consummated in the "marital act"—i.e., sex. It is not far off the mark to call marriage "the sacrament of sex."

The crucial difference between the pagan view of sexuality found in *The Da Vinci Code* and the Christian view is not that pagans think sex is sacred and Christians think it is dirty. Rather, the difference is that paganism, as ever, gets it backward by worshiping the creature rather than the Creator. Saying that Jesus was about sex, as Brown implies, is getting it backward. In fact, *sex* is about *Jesus*, for He is the creator of sex. He is the eternal Bridegroom in the great Cosmic Marriage with His Bride, the Church. Our earthly experience of marriage is but a foreshadowing of the heavenly reality of our union with Christ. For the pagan, heaven is the shadow: the earthly experience of sex is the reality.

Christian marriage insists on the privacy of the sexual act because it is our most powerful earthly experience of intimacy and it images the intimacy of God's relationship with the soul. But for pagans, sex is made a public act before spectators because the participants are emptied of their individuality and made into icons through which worshipers ritually participate in an abstraction called the "sacred masculine" and the "sacred feminine." Like so much else in paganism, this turns the natural order of things on its head.

In Christianity, the place for the *public* sacramental celebration of the union between God and His worshipers is the holy Eucharist, not marriage. There, it is fitting for the priest to lose his individuality and stand in as "another Christ" as the congregation is joined in union with God through reception of the body and blood of Jesus Christ. But in marriage, what is vital is that two people who are completely themselves come together in love and intimacy. While it is true that the community as a whole benefits greatly from this union, the principal recipients of the grace of marriage are the husband and wife themselves. In marriage, they experience something of the love that exists between Jesus and His Church and they thereby complete one another in grace.

49. **Did the ancient Jews really believe that their Temple housed not only the male God, YHWH, but also his female counterpart, *Shekinah*, as *The Da Vinci Code* claims?**

One of the things that makes Judaism stand out in a particular way among all the religions in the ancient

Near East is its strong monotheistic emphasis. While many of the pagan religions surrounding the Israelite people had male and female gods paired up, ancient orthodox Jews would have shuddered at the thought of YHWH—the one true God over all creation—having a female consort or wife like some pagan deities did.

Yet *The Da Vinci Code* makes the very strange assertion that the Jews believed YHWH had a "powerful feminine equal" named *Shekinah*. In reality, however, the word *shekinah* was never used in ancient Judaism to describe a female goddess. It referred instead to the manifestation of YHWH's presence on earth. Thought not found in the Bible, *shekinah* was a theological term used by ancient Jewish rabbis to describe God's glory dwelling in the tabernacle or Temple. The notion that the word refers to a female consort such that ancient orthodox Jews believed in a male deity called YHWH and a female deity called *Shekinah* is completely unfounded.

CHAPTER 8

BLUNDERS AND LIES ABOUT CONSTANTINE AND THE COUNCIL OF NICEA

50. Who was Constantine?

Constantine was the Roman emperor who legalized Christianity in A.D. 313. Until his reign, Christians had been subject to sporadic persecution, culminating in a catastrophic and deadly empire-wide pogrom under his predecessor, Diocletian. Just before a crucial battle, Constantine reportedly had a vision in which he was shown the sign of the cross in the sky and told by an inner voice, "By this sign, conquer." Constantine ordered a cross placed on the shields of his troops and went on to win the battle. Concluding that the Christian God had helped him, he subsequently issued the Edict of Toleration at Milan and began a life-long friendship with the Church.

Constantine was an emperor, not a theologian. His primary concern was peace throughout the Empire. When theological controversies arose about the exact nature of Jesus and threatened the peace of his empire, he demanded that the bishops of the Church meet to resolve the controversy. At the same time, he was not particular about the details of the controversy. He simply wanted it resolved so that peace would return to the Empire. That's the basic historical background to the Council of Nicea—a council that had absolutely nothing to do with settling the canon of Scripture or with turning Jesus from a "mortal prophet" into God.

51. Didn't Constantine commission a new Bible and outlaw all the other "gospels"?

In about A.D. 320, Constantine did commission fifty copies of the Bible to be made in order to promote Christian worship in the churches of the capital. But it is misleading to say he commissioned a *new* Bible. Constantine did not decide for the Church which books were to be included in the New Testament. That issue was largely settled during the two centuries before his reign. As we will see, the list of the four gospels was for the most part fixed by A.D. 200, and there was substantial agreement about most of the New Testament books by the end of the 200s—long before Constantine ordered that copies of the Bible be made. Constantine simply brought together many of the Scriptures Christians throughout the world were already using for their prayer, worship, and teaching. The fifty bibles he commissioned did not omit or embellish any of the accepted gospels. And, while the authority of a few other New Testament books were still being debated in the time of Constantine (e.g., the book of Revelation), there were no major differences between the New Testament manuscripts copied before the time of Constantine and the manuscripts that were handed on afterward.

52. But didn't Constantine suppress the earlier Gnostic gospels that spoke of Christ's human traits in favor of the gospels that portray Him as more God-like?

First, keep in mind that the Gnostic gospels were *not* the "earlier" gospels. The oldest Gnostic gospels were written generations after the life of Jesus, and most of the Gnostic texts come from at least a century or two later—long after the writing of the New Testament documents, which were composed in the time of the apostles, ranging from perhaps the middle to the end of the first century. This means that the distance in time between the New Testament documents and the events of Jesus' life is about the same as that between ourselves and the events of World War II through the Carter Administration. The gap, though, between the Gnostic gospels and Jesus is similar to the time between us and the Civil War, at best.

Second, if Constantine or the Catholic Church were trying to suppress gospels that spoke of Christ's human traits, they should have gotten rid of Matthew, Mark, Luke, and John, for these gospels clearly present the humanity of Jesus. The four canonical gospels show that Jesus has real flesh and blood. He gets hungry and thirsty. He eats, drinks, talks, prays, sleeps, and weeps. He increases in wisdom and stature as He grows from a child to a man. He even suffers and dies. He also associates with other human beings, visiting people's homes, sharing meals, having conversations, and showing compassion in their sufferings. If, as *The Da Vinci Code* claims, there were a conspiracy to suppress Christ's humanity, it's hard to imagine why so many of Christ's human traits were left in the four gospels!

Third, the Gnostic gospels do not highlight Jesus' humanity nearly as well as the four New Testament gospels do. In many passages in the Gnostic gospels, one does not get a clear picture of the flesh-and-blood Jesus as an historical figure interacting in the real world of first century Judaism. Instead, Jesus is often portrayed as a timeless, abstract, esoteric teacher, whose ordinary human qualities are not emphasized. In some Gnostic texts, it is not at all clear whether Jesus really was a human being in a human body. For example, according to the *Acts of John*, Jesus seems to have a phantom-like appearance rather than a real human body. He does not leave footprints on the ground, and He does not even blink. The *Apocalypse of Peter* claims that Jesus Himself did not really die on the Cross. The Living Jesus was above the Cross laughing at His persecutors while they crucified "His fleshly part, which is the substitute." Similarly, in the *Second Treatise of the Great Seth*, the spiritual Jesus says He did not wear the crown of thorns, drink the vinegar, carry the Cross, or die on Calvary. Jesus appears in this text as too spiritual to suffer and die like a human being. In fact, He is quoted as saying, "I did not die in reality, but in appearance."

In sum, the Gnostic "gospels" do not leave us with a more human Jesus. Rather, we find in these passages a ghostly and ethereal Jesus who is far removed from our own humanity, unlike the real Jesus found in Matthew, Mark, Luke, and John. Thus, the claims of *The Da Vinci Code* on this point are exactly opposite of what the Gnostic texts actually say about Jesus.

53. While we're talking about the Gnostic gospels, what is Gnosticism anyway?

Gnosticism was an ancient Greek religious movement that influenced the thought of some Christians in the early Church, leading to several beliefs out of harmony with the Christian tradition handed down from the apostles. While there were many different strands and expressions of Gnosticism in the early Church, some common Gnostic themes include the belief that: only the spiritual world is good and the material world is bad; the human soul is imprisoned in the evil body; salvation consists of the soul being released from the body through secret knowledge (*gnosis* means "knowledge" in Greek); and only a few receive this secret knowledge about God.

54. *The Da Vinci Code* asserts that before the Council of Nicea in A.D. 325, Christians believed Jesus was just a man, not the divine Son of God. Is this true?

This may be the most misleading "fact" in the entire novel. The earliest Christians believed Jesus was the divine Son of God from the very beginning—*centuries* before the Council of Nicea. All one has to do is look at the New Testament or even the writings of the Church Fathers, and it is abundantly clear that many Christians in the first three centuries believed Jesus was the "Son of God" and divine.

More than 250 years before the Council of Nicea, Jesus was recognized as the "Son of God" in the writings of the New Testament. Paul's letters alone refer to Jesus as the "Son of God" seventeen times, and the New Testament as a whole refers to Him as God's Son *more than 100 times*. This popular biblical title for Jesus is repeated often throughout the writings of the early Christian tradition.

As for Christ's divinity, consider the following New Testament texts, all of which show how their writers believed Jesus to be divine: the gospel of Mark testifies to a belief in Christ's divinity when it narrates how Jesus does something only God can do—forgive sins on His own authority. Jesus is immediately charged with blasphemy because the people say only God can forgive sin (Mark 2:1-12). In John's gospel, Jesus is reported to have said, "I and the Father are one" (John 10:30). The text goes on to tell us that Jesus is not claiming to have a vague spiritual unity with the Father, but that He is putting Himself on par with God. The Jews accuse Jesus of blasphemy and attempt to stone Him, saying, "...you being a man make yourself God." Similarly, Jesus uses the sacred name of God—I AM (*Yahweh*)—that was revealed to Moses at the burning bush (Exodus 3:13-14). In the Jewish tradition, the divine name was so holy, it was never spoken (except by the high priest during the sacred rites of the Day of Atonement). Jesus, however, not only speaks the unutterable, holy name of God, but He applies it to Himself, saying: "Before Abraham was, I AM" (John 8:58). And once again, His fellow Jews want to stone Him for this. These and many other passages demonstrate how the New Testament reflects belief in Christ's divinity from the very dawn of the Christian era.

In the century following the writing of the New Testament, the writings of the early Christians continued to give strong testimony to Christ's divinity. In A.D. 107, Ignatius of Antioch referred to Jesus as "God" and "man" and "our God, Jesus Christ." In A.D. 150, Justin Martyr wrote that Jesus "was God, the Son of the only unbegotten, unutterable God." In A.D. 177, Irenaeus described Jesus as "true man" and "true God." And around the year 200, Tertullian wrote that, in Jesus, "We see a two-fold state, not confused, but united in a single person, Jesus, God and man." While some of the details on precisely *how* Christ's divinity relates to His humanity were still being worked out, there is abundant evidence for belief in Christ's divinity in the first and second centuries of the Christian era—that's more than 100 to 200 years before the Council of Nicea!

55. But *The Da Vinci Code* says the Council of Nicea gave the human Jesus an "upgrade" by establishing Him as "the Son of God."

Once again, *The Da Vinci Code* does not get even the most basic historical facts straight, for the Council of Nicea was not even about *whether* Jesus was the Son of God. As mentioned previously, Jesus' divinity was already an established Christian belief. Nicea addressed the teaching of a priest named Arius, who recognized Jesus as the Son of God, the first-born of all creation, and the mediator through whom the Father created all things. Arius, like nearly all Christians in the first three centuries of Christianity, had no problem referring to Jesus as the "Son of God." He just didn't believe Jesus was *always* the Son, and that got him into trouble. Arius taught that there was a time when the Son did not exist. God created the Son and then adopted Him. Therefore, in Arius' view, Jesus is not fully divine with the Father. The Council of Nicea rightly condemned Arius' teaching, for it ends up denying the long-held Christian belief in Christ's divinity. Notice, though, that compared to *The Da Vinci Code*, Arius is practically a Catholic. For him, and for all the bishops at the Council, Jesus is vastly more than a mere "mortal prophet." The quarrel at Nicea was never between those who saw Jesus as a mere man and those who saw Him as divine. It was between those who saw Him as a mighty supernatural creature second only to God (i.e., Arius and his followers) and those who insisted that He was Himself God (i.e., orthodox Christian believers).

56. So what *did* the Council of Nicea teach?

The Council of Nicea affirmed Christ's divinity as the eternal Son of God. The Council issued the famous statement of faith commonly known as "the Nicene Creed," which Catholics recite every Sunday at Mass. Countering Arius' teaching that the Son is a lower being than the Father, the Nicene Creed emphasizes that the Son is equally divine with the Father: He is "God from God, light from light, true God from true God." In opposition to Arius' teaching that there was a time when the Son did not exist and that the Son was then created by the Father, the Nicene Creed says the Son was "begotten, not made"—meaning the Son is eternally begotten of the Father, not something the Father created like He did the angels, the sun, or the animals. Finally, this Creed says the Son is "one in being with the Father"—meaning that the Son is fully divine, of the same substance as the Father.

57. ***The Da Vinci Code* says Christ's establishment as the Son of God was the result of a "relatively close vote" at the Council of Nicea. Is this true?**

No, it's dead wrong in more ways than one. As we have already seen, Christians believed in Christ's divinity and His being the Son of God from the very beginning—centuries before the Council of Nicea in A.D. 325. The Council was called to address particular questions about the nature of Christ's divine Sonship that were raised by Arius' teachings. And there was little support at Nicea for Arius' diminished view of Christ.

As for the "closeness" of the vote concerning Christ's nature, there were at least 220 bishops at the Council of Nicea. Only *two* voted in favor of Arius' position!   The rest—more than 99 percent of the bishops—voted against Arius, in favor of the belief that Jesus was fully divine and equal with the Father. Therefore, at best, the score at Nicea was 218–2.   Hardly "a close vote." And not even a vote about whether Jesus was a merely a "mortal prophet."

58. **Why does Brown say the Vatican used the Council of Nicea to solidify its grip on power when Constantine called the Council and transferred the seat of power from Rome to Constantinople?**

On this point, Brown is again either extremely ignorant or extremely dishonest about the elementary facts of history because there was no "Vatican" in Constantine's day. The area that is now Vatican City was a swamp, and the Church of Rome, though home to the pope, was located in a city of declining political significance. That's why Constantine transferred the capital of the Empire to Constantinople (modern-day Istanbul, Turkey), where it would continue as the capital of the Byzantine empire for another thousand years after the fall of Rome to barbarians in A.D. 476.

One thing to be aware of in reading *The Da Vinci Code* is that, for Brown, "the Vatican" is practically synonymous with the Catholic Church. Consequently, he will make all sorts of ridiculous claims about Constantine's alleged schemes to "solidify the Vatican power base" despite the fact that the Vatican did not come into existence until Constantine had been in his grave for more than 800 years.

CHAPTER 9

THE RELIABILITY OF SCRIPTURE

59. ***The Da Vinci Code* seems to challenge the Bible a lot. The book says "the Bible did not arrive by fax from heaven" and that it is a product of man. Doesn't that downgrade the Scriptures into ordinary human documents?**

The Da Vinci Code's announcement that the Bible was not faxed from heaven in complete bound copies is somehow supposed to be startling new information that will shake the faith of Christian believers. But this fact is not news at all. Christianity has always recognized that humans were involved in the production of the Bible and that men such as Matthew, Mark, Peter, and Paul composed the sacred books and acted as true authors under divine inspiration. And this human involvement in the writing of the Scriptures has never been seen by Christians as taking away from the sacredness of the biblical text.

In addition, *The Da Vinci Code* is not presenting the whole truth when it says the Bible is a product of man. It fails to mention God's involvement in the process. Christians have always believed that the Bible is *inspired*—a word that literally means, "God-breathed" (1 Timothy 3:15). In other words, God influenced the human writers and "breathed"

His own Word through the words of men in the Scriptures.

Therefore, the Bible is like Jesus Christ: fully human *and* fully divine. The human writers made full use of their own freedom, creativity, and writing style to communicate their message to their audience. But the mystery of divine inspiration is that precisely through each human author's own particular personality, freedom, and skills, God communicated exactly what He wanted written in the books of the Bible (see *Catechism of the Catholic Church*, paragraph 106). *The Da Vinci Code* completely misses this point. It emphasizes only the human aspect of the Bible, and, in doing so, misleads the reader by excluding God's involvement in the process.

60. But do you really believe God inspired human beings to write the Bible?

Absolutely! It is understandable, though, that some may find the idea of God inspiring human writers to author the Bible difficult to grasp. This is probably because these same people do not believe God has much interaction with the world. So, if one doesn't believe God can perform miracles, hear prayers, or interact with the natural world at all, then, of course, he or she is not going to be very open-minded to the possibility of God communicating Himself through the Bible.

But it simply doesn't make sense to limit God in this radical way. If God created the universe, then He is certainly capable of acting within the very world He made. Thus, we should be open to the fact that God *can* hear our prayers, influence affairs on earth, work miracles, and communicate to us through the inspired books of the Bible.

Furthermore, it makes sense that God would communicate with us. After all, we need His help to understand Him and His plan for our lives. Our finite minds by themselves cannot fully grasp the infinite God. Many of us have a hard enough time understanding the things of this world, such as physics, calculus, or molecular biology. If we experience difficulty understanding such earthy matters, why should we be surprised that our limited minds cannot understand God? If God is infinite and our minds are not, it seems fitting that God would reveal Himself to us and communicate His will to us so that we could know Him, love Him, and serve Him more fully. This is what He has done in the Bible.

61. But the *Da Vinci Code* says the Bible evolved through countless additions and revisions. After all, there weren't printing presses or copy machines in the ancient world. How do we know that the New Testament we have today is an accurate representation of the original New Testament?

The New Testament we have today is not only trustworthy, its books are by far the most reliable texts we have from the ancient world. The sheer number of ancient manuscript copies of the New Testament books is impressive. And some of these copies are very ancient, very close to when the original manuscripts were composed.

To better illustrate this point, let's compare the New Testament manuscript tradition to the *second* best attested work in antiquity: *The Iliad,* the ancient Greek epic by Homer. Homer wrote *The Iliad* around 800 B.C., but we have no original manuscript of the work. Our modern day editions of this classical work are based on manuscripts that date from long after Homer's lifetime. Of the approximately 650 extant manuscripts of *The Iliad,* the oldest dates from around A.D. 200 to 300—about 1,000 years after Homer's lifetime! Nevertheless, most scholars recognize that these very late copies of *The Iliad* are reliable representations of Homer's original work, even though they date from more than a millennium after Homer himself.

The New Testament has a much stronger manuscript tradition than *The Iliad.* First, there are many more ancient manuscripts of the New Testament: we have well over 5,000 manuscript copies of the New Testament in whole or in part. Second, these manuscripts are much closer in date to the originals. The New Testament was written within the first century A.D., and we have copies of some of those New Testament writings within just a few decades after they were composed.

We have fragments and major portions of individual New Testament books dating from the second and third centuries A.D. And we have bound copies of the entire New Testament from the fourth and fifth centuries. So there are only 200 to 300 years between the copies and their original manuscripts. But with the very reliable *Iliad,* there's a 1,000 year gap between Homer and the earliest extant copies of the work. Therefore, the New Testament has a much stronger manuscript history than any other writings of the ancient world.

62. OK. But how do we know these New Testament manuscripts faithfully represent the original text?

Because when you place the 5,000 or so existing New Testament manuscripts side-by-side, they match up almost perfectly. It's important to note that these manuscripts were copied by many different people, from various parts of the world, at different times. Yet scholars have shown how these 5,000 copies are a 99.5 percent match with each other on all major points. There may be some minor variations in terms of spelling, word order, or vocabulary, but nothing that changes the sense of a particular verse or passage—nothing affecting matters of doctrine or morals.

This remarkably low rate of variation between the thousands of New Testament manuscripts should not surprise us. Remember, the early Christians who passed on the Scriptures were copying the sacred texts they used for teaching, prayer, and worship. Indeed, they believed they were copying the very Word of God Himself. These manuscripts were copied with great care and reverence. In sum, the New Testament is the most reliable text we have from antiquity. As Evangelical scholars Norman Geisler and William Nix explain: "The New Testament, then, has not only survived in more manuscripts than any other book from antiquity, but it has survived in a purer form than any other great book—a form that is 99.5 percent pure." If the New Testament is not trustworthy, then no writings from the ancient world can be considered reliable —not Cicero, not Homer, not Plato, not Caesar. If we can't trust the New Testament manuscript tradition, then all university history and classics departments across the country should be shut down because they have no reliable documents from which to teach!

CHAPTER 10

THE CANON OF SCRIPTURE

63. Who determined which books would be part of the New Testament?

In the end, the Catholic Church determined which books would be part of the New Testament. But let's take a look at the beginning of the story: While the Jewish Old Testament books were revered as Scripture in the early Church, the first generation of Christians began composing their own writings by the middle of the first century A.D., within the first generation of Christianity. Many of these writings, such as the letters of Paul and the four Gospels, were copied and shared with other Christian communities, and they grew in use and esteem as Christianity spread throughout the world. Although there were many Christian texts written and circulated in the first three centuries, the ones that were in harmony with the standard beliefs of the Christian faith and that proved to be, over time, the most useful for preaching, teaching, and worship gained the widest acceptance in the early Church.

We see a basic level of acceptance for many of the New Testament books already within the first two centuries of Christianity in the writings of the most respected Christian leaders of this period. Many of these bishops and theologians (known as the

Church Fathers)—who were writing in the second, third, and fourth centuries—either explicitly quote from or allude to ideas from the four gospels, the letters of Paul, and other writings that came to be part of the New Testament. Furthermore, in the late second and third centuries, these Church Fathers began clarifying which of the Christian texts they considered to be most authoritative, and they started developing lists of the official New Testament books.

By the fourth century, the collection of New Testament books became fixed with the same twenty-seven books we have in our Bibles today. In A.D. 367, Athanasius, the bishop of Alexandria, lists these twenty-seven books—and these alone—as the authoritative Christian writings that could be read at Mass. This same list of twenty-seven New Testament books was given by a wider group of bishops at two councils in the early Church, the Council of Hippo in A.D. 393 and the Council of Carthage in 397. This list of twenty-seven books was reaffirmed in a definitive manner by the Council of Trent in the 16th century. And all Christians—both Catholic and Protestant alike—revere these same twenty-seven books as being divinely inspired and part of the "canon" of Scripture.

64. **But what criteria did the Church follow when deciding which books should be included in the New Testament?**

The twenty-seven books of the New Testament gained widespread acceptance in the early Church and were confirmed as being part of the inspired Scriptures for several reasons:

1) These books were rooted in the *apostolic tradition*. They were written either by one of the apostles themselves (e.g., Matthew, John) or by a disciple or coworker of an apostle (e.g., Mark was a disciple of Peter, and Luke was a disciple of Paul).

2) They were known for their *catholicity* (or "universality"). In other words, they had relevance not just for one particular community or region of the Church, but they were applicable to and revered by Christians throughout the world.

3) They were considered *orthodox*, meaning they were in harmony with the teachings of the apostles. No writing could be considered authoritative if it was not in harmony with the Church's teaching, especially as it is summed up in the Creed. For example, a bishop in Antioch banned the Gospel of Peter from being used because it denied the humanity of Christ.

   The irony of Brown's claim that there was some "great Catholic conspiracy" to cover up Jesus' humanity is that he gets it backward. The critical issue for the New Testament writers and the leaders of the early Church was not to persuade people Jesus was divine, but to continually remind them that He was truly *human*. John, in his first letter, had to go so far as to warn that if any teacher denies Jesus has come in the flesh, he is speaking in the spirit of the antichrist (see 1 John 4:1-3).

4) They were *used in the sacred liturgy*, i.e., these books were not simply used for spiritual

reading and teaching, but were also used for divine worship in the Mass.

65. Who gave the bishops of the Catholic Church the authority to make these decisions about the New Testament?

Jesus Himself. Both the New Testament and the writings of the early Christians make it abundantly clear that Christ gave His authority to the apostles and their successors to teach and lead the Church in His name.

First, the New Testament highlights that Jesus chose twelve apostles and gave them authority to teach, heal, and act in His name. "And he called the twelve together and gave them power and authority over all demons and to cure diseases, and he sent them out to preach the kingdom of God and to heal" (Luke 9:1-2). After His resurrection, Jesus entrusted the apostles with the same mission He received from His heavenly Father. "As the Father sent me, even so I send you" (John 20:21). Before ascending into heaven, Jesus gave the apostles authority to baptize, teach, and make disciples of all nations, and promised that He would always be with them in this mission (Matthew 28:18-20). Here we see that the apostles were not simply important Church leaders who should be respected and followed. They were much more than that. They were "ministers of a new covenant" (2 Corinthians 3:6), "ambassadors for Christ" (2 Corinthians 5:20) and "servants of Christ and stewards of the mysteries of God" (1 Corinthians 4:1). In other words, the apostles represented Jesus Christ and taught in His name.

Jesus put such a close identification between the apostles' teachings and His own teaching that He told them, "He who hears you hears me, and he who rejects you rejects me, and he who rejects me rejects him who sent me" (Luke 10:16). Did you catch that? Listening to the apostles is listening to Christ. No one in the first century could say to Jesus, "I want to follow you and your teachings, but I don't want to accept your apostles' teachings." To reject the teachings of the apostles is to reject Jesus Christ Himself.

Second, the apostles in turn passed on this authority to other men who would carry out Christ's mission. Like the apostles themselves, these successors (i.e., the bishops) do not take the place of Christ but represent Him. They teach not on their own authority but with the authority of Christ Himself. The importance of the apostles' successors, the bishops, was already well-known in the first decades of the Church. St. Paul writes about the office of bishop (1 Timothy 3:1-7), noting that a bishop must hold firm to the Gospel that has been passed on to him because he has the special role of faithfully teaching the "sound doctrine" that he received and of guarding it against skewed interpretations and attacks from those who oppose it (Titus 1:7-9).

Then, in the first generation of Christians after the apostles, the third bishop of Rome, Clement, teaches very clearly about how the authority Christ entrusted to the apostles was now being handed over to the apostles' successors. In his letter to the Corinthians, written around A.D. 96, Clement says the apostles "appointed their first converts, after testing them by the Spirit, to be bishops and deacons for the believers of the future. This was in no way an innovation, for bishops and deacons had already been spoken of in Scripture long before that." Similarly, another early Church Father named Ignatius, who was bishop of Antioch, calls on Christians to follow the authority of the bishops as if they were following Christ. In a letter from around A.D. 107, Ignatius warns the Christians in Tralles to obey their bishop as if he were Christ and to "never act independently of the bishop." He develops this theme even more in his letter to the Christians in Smyrna, which says: "Follow your bishop, every one of you, as obediently as Jesus Christ followed the Father. Obey your clergy too, as you would the Apostles ... Make sure that no step affecting the church is ever taken by anyone without the bishop's sanction ... Where the bishop is seen, there let all his people be; just as wherever Jesus is present, we have the catholic Church."

The earliest Christians clearly saw the need to follow the leadership and teaching authority of the bishops, united with the successor of Peter, the bishop of Rome. So if the bishops of the early Church officially taught which books were part of the New Testament, we should accept that teaching not simply because it makes sense (which it does, based on the criteria discussed earlier), but because these bishops taught with the authority of Christ. Without the authority of Jesus Christ entrusted to the Catholic Church, we would never know for sure which books were inspired. As St. Augustine once said, "I would not believe in the Gospel if the authority of the Catholic Church did not move me to do so."

CHAPTER 11

THE FOUR GOSPELS OR THE GNOSTIC GOSPELS?

66. *The Da Vinci Code* **says the Dead Sea Scrolls and the Nag Hammadi scrolls—not the books of the New Testament—are "the earliest Christian records." Is this right? What are these writings anyway?**

This is yet another example of how *The Da Vinci Code* cannot get even the most basic historical facts right. The Dead Sea scrolls are not *Christian* records at all—they are *Jewish* ones! They are a collection of about 850 manuscripts from a group of early Jews known as the Essenes. This ascetic sect lived at Qumran near the Dead Sea between the second century B.C. and the first century A.D., and the scrolls themselves were discovered in caves in that area in 1947. No Christian documents have ever been found there, and the Dead Sea scrolls themselves make no mention of Jesus or Christianity. They are entirely *Jewish* texts. To say the Dead Sea scrolls are some of "the earliest Christian records" is as erroneous as saying the Declaration of Independence is one of the earliest British documents—not just wrong, but profoundly confused.

The Nag Hammadi scrolls were found in 1945 near the town of Nag Hammadi in Egypt. They consist of more than fifty texts representing the largest and most important collection of Gnostic writings.

Revered in *The Da Vinci Code,* these scrolls contain many strange Gnostic ideas not found in the earliest Christian writings.

Scholars believe most of the Nag Hammadi documents are copies of texts originally written in the third and fourth centuries A.D., though some argue that a few of the texts may date from as early as A.D. 150. Still, even accepting this earlier date, the year 150 is much later than the writing of the New Testament texts. Virtually all scholars—Christian and non-Christian alike—recognize that the New Testament itself was written within the first century, with some of Paul's letters being written as early as AD 50—100 years *before* the earliest Nag Hammadi texts. Thus, the Nag Hammadi scrolls certainly are *not* "the earliest Christian records" since they come generations after the writings of Paul and the gospels.

67. **But *The Da Vinci Code* claims there were "more than *eighty* gospels" considered for the New Testament, and that only Matthew, Mark, Luke, and John were chosen. Is that true?**

Here, Brown tries to get readers to think that the Gnostics and other groups wrote about eighty different "gospels," and that these "gospels" were rivals to Matthew, Mark, Luke, and John. But there were no where near eighty "gospels" floating around the early Church. Just consider the Nag Hammadi scrolls themselves, which *The Da Vinci Code* goes on to mention after making this outlandish claim. If you were to go to your local library and find the English edition of *The Nag Hammadi Library*, you would see that the Nag Hammadi scrolls themselves consist of only forty-five different titles. And of these forty-five writings, only *five* are actually called "gospels."

Furthermore, within the first century after the apostles, the Church already recognized the gospels of Matthew, Mark, Luke, and John as authoritative writings inspired by the Holy Spirit and part of the New Testament canon. For example, before A.D. 125, when an early Church bishop named Papias wrote about how the words and deeds of Jesus were passed on from the apostles to him, he mentions three of the New Testament gospels (Matthew, Mark, and John)— but none of the Gnostic gospels. Similarly, when Tatian in the year A.D. 170 compiles the different gospel accounts into one harmonized text, he synthesizes Matthew, Mark, Luke, and John—but not any of the Gnostic gospels. By the end of the second century, the four-fold Gospel is largely fixed in the Christian tradition, so much so that Irenaeus in A.D. 177 can write that the four gospels of Matthew, Mark, Luke, and John are an established fact as much as the four corners of the world and the four winds:

> As there are four quarters of the world in which we live, and four universal winds, and as the church is dispersed over all the earth, and the Gospel is the pillar and base of the church, so it is natural that it should have four pillars, breathing immortality from every quarter and kindling human life anew. Clearly therefore the Word ... having been made manifest to the human race, has given us the gospel in fourfold form, but held together by one Spirit (*Adversus Haereses* ["Against Heresies"], III)

68. I'd never heard of the Gnostic gospels before I read *The Da Vinci Code*. Are they being kept secret by the Catholic Church?

The Da Vinci Code tries to get its readers to think that they are being let in on a big secret that has been kept hidden from the public: namely, that alternative gospel accounts from early Christianity have been discovered and the Catholic Church doesn't want you to know about it! In reality, though, the discovery of the Nag Hammadi writings is very old news that received media attention decades ago. The texts themselves were made available to the general public shortly after their discovery in 1945. An English translation of one of the most popular texts from these scrolls, the *Gospel of Thomas*, was published in 1959. And these writings gained further popular attention in the late 1970s when the first complete English translation, *The Nag Hammadi Library,* was made available, and the ideas in these scrolls were popularized in Elaine Pagels' 1979 book, *The Gnostic Gospels*. No secrets here! Public interest in the Nag Hammadi documents is older than disco. Just go to any large bookstore and you could pick up a copy of these texts for yourself. You can even read the Nag Hammadi writings on-line at The Gnostic Society Library website: www. gnosis.org/naghamm/nhl.html

69. Still, the 1945 discovery of the Nag Hammadi scrolls must have come as a shock to the Catholic Church. What will the Church do now that people finally know about Gnostic Christianity and its scriptures?

Actually, the fact that there were Gnostic Christians and Gnostic writings in the early Church had been widely known for centuries—long before the discovery of the Nag Hammadi scrolls. In fact, more than 1,700 years before the 1945 Nag Hammadi find, Church Fathers such as Irenaeus, Hippolytus, and Tertullian combated Gnostic ideas in their own writings. In the course of their arguments, they thoroughly described Gnostic beliefs and practices in order to refute them, thereby providing us with many details about certain Gnostic groups, beliefs, and writings. Thus, the modern world first came to know of these Gnostic writings primarily through the Catholic Church. (By the way, the discovery of the Nag Hammadi scrolls bears out the descriptions of Gnostic beliefs we have from the Church Fathers, giving the lie to yet another *Da Vinci* myth: the notion that "History is written by the winners to make the losers look bad.")

Furthermore, portions of some actual Gnostic writings such as the *Gospel of Thomas* and a work called *Pistis Sophia* were discovered over a century ago, between 1880 and 1920. Some of these works were translated into English, and many of their ideas reached large audiences through magazines, newspapers, and other popular literature. For example, consider the landmark 1924 publication *The Apocryphal New Testament*, in which the editor, Montague James, offered a comprehensive English translation of many of the Gnostic texts and other apocryphal writings that were known at the time. In the preface, James notes how well-known these texts had already become: "It is a matter of common knowledge that there exist such things as Apocryphal Gospels, Acts, Epistles, Revelations ... Bible dictionaries, encyclopedias, manuals, and textbooks have made the fact familiar. Moreover without much trouble, it is possible for the less incurious to get hold of translations of a good many of these books" (see Montague James, trans.,

The Apocryphal New Testament, Clarendon Press, 1924, p. *xi*). So way back in the early 1920s—well before the Nag Hammadi discoveries in 1945, and even longer before *The Da Vinci Code's* publication in 2003—an authority like Montague James speaks of the Gnostic and apocryphal writings as "common knowledge," and he notes how the average person could easily access an English translation of many of these texts.

The Nag Hammadi scrolls may have given us more documents and a fuller picture of some Gnostic thought. But the existence of these Gnostic groups and their writings was not as dramatically secretive as *The Da Vinci Code* would like us to believe. Some of the views and writings of these Gnostic-like groups have been known for well over a millennium through the writings of the Church Fathers. And portions of these texts were discovered and made public nearly a century ago.

Besides, these Gnostic documents don't give us any revolutionary insights into who Jesus really was. Most were written 100 to 300 years after Jesus' earthly life—that's as far removed from the world of Jesus as we are today from the worlds of Abraham Lincoln and George Washington. And they were written much later than the four original gospels which were composed within a few decades after Christ, when many eyewitnesses to His words and deeds were still alive. Certainly, accounts from the first generation of Christianity are bound to give us a lot more historical evidence about Jesus than accounts of Gnostic-like fringe groups coming centuries after His lifetime.

CHAPTER 12

MARY MAGDALENE

70. Mary Magdalene comes up a lot in *The Da Vinci Code*. What does the Bible tell us about this woman?

Mary Magdalene is introduced in the gospel of Luke as a follower of Jesus who had seven demons cast out of her. She became part of a group of women who provided for Christ and the apostles out of their own means and traveled with them during their ministry (Luke 8:1-3). She followed Jesus all the way to Jerusalem and was present at key moments surrounding His death and resurrection. She was a witness to Christ's crucifixion on Calvary (Matthew 27:56), she was present at His burial (Matthew 27:61), and she was the first witness to His resurrection. The gospels tell us that on Easter Sunday, Mary went with some other women to Christ's tomb, bringing spices to anoint His body, but they found the tomb empty (Mark 16:1, Luke 24:1-2). According to Luke, the women saw two angelic figures in dazzling apparel who told them that Jesus had risen from the dead. And Mary Magdalene was among the women who went to tell the apostles of these dramatic events (Luke 24:3-10). John's gospel gives us the account of the most amazing thing that happened to Mary Magdalene on Easter: she became the first person to encounter the risen Jesus Himself. In John 20:11-18, Jesus appeared to Mary near the tomb while she was weeping. At first, she did not recognize Him. But after Jesus called her name, Mary realized it was Him, clung to Him, and was instructed to tell the apostles that He was ascending the Father. Mary obediently carried out Christ's command, saying to the apostles, "I have seen the Lord" and telling them all He said to her (John 20:18).

71.   Many people think that Mary Magdalene was a prostitute. Does the Bible teach this?

As far as Mary Magdalene's past goes, the Bible tells us only that she had seven demons cast out of her (Luke 8:2). Since seven is the biblical number of perfection (or completion), the fact that Mary had seven demons indicates the severity of her past demonic possession. However, the Bible nowhere describes Mary's past in detail or says she was a prostitute.

One of the first people we know to link Mary Magdalene with prostitution was Pope Gregory the Great in a homily he gave in A.D. 591. In this homily, Gregory identifies Mary Magdalene with the unnamed sinful woman who anoints Christ's feet in Luke 7:36-50. The way Luke describes this repentant woman ("a woman of the city, who was a sinner") indicates that she was likely a prostitute. But why might Gregory identify this sinful woman with Mary Magdalene? First, the story of the unnamed sinner in Luke 7 comes immediately before the passage in which Mary Magdalene is introduced by name in Luke 8. Second, Mary

Magdalene's hometown of Magdala had a bad reputation for its immorality and licentiousness. This may have further supported the association of Mary Magdalene and prostitution.

This interpretation of Mary Magdalene as the repentant prostitute of Luke 7 became widespread in Western Christianity. It didn't catch on in the East, though, which viewed the unnamed woman and Mary Magdalene as two separate individuals. While there is no biblical obstacle to the traditional Western view of Mary as a prostitute, there is no definitive biblical proof for it either. This may be one reason why, in 1969, when the Catholic Church revised the order of Bible readings used at Mass, it decided to no longer use the account of the unnamed repentant sinner in Luke 7 as a reading on the feast of St. Mary Magdalene—thus, clearly leaving open the question of the identity of the woman about whom Luke is writing.

72. So *The Da Vinci Code* is right when it says the Catholic Church led a "smear campaign" against Mary Magdalene, slandering her by turning her into a prostitute.

No, the Catholic Church honors Mary Magdalene *as a saint!* She has her own feast day in the liturgical calendar. Catholics often turn to Mary Magdalene in prayer, asking her to pray for them. Churches throughout the world have been named after her. Countless statues, stained glass windows, and paintings depict her holiness. Christians have made pilgrimages to pray at places where her relics were believed to be kept. Does any of this sound anything like "a smear campaign"? In the Catholic tradition, Mary Magdalene is recognized as one of the most important women who followed Jesus. She is called "the apostle to the apostles," for she was the first to announce the risen Christ to the apostles on Easter Sunday. And she is hailed as the first witness to the Resurrection. If the Catholic Church was maliciously trying to erase the memory of Mary Magdalene as an important, holy follower of Jesus Christ, it did an absolutely horrible job. What Brown alleges to be a smear campaign in the Catholic Church has turned out to be a 2,000-year-long celebration honoring Mary Magdalene as one of the greatest saints in the Bible.

As for Pope Gregory the Great's association of Mary Magdalene with prostitution, we must remember the context in which he made this connection. It was in a homily at one church in Rome—not in an authoritative papal teaching intended to be binding on all the Catholic faithful. His main focus in this homily was not to give a scholarly historical analysis of Mary Magdalene's identity but to give a spiritual, allegorical interpretation of the unnamed sinful woman of Luke 7 and Mary Magdalene in Luke 8 in order to inspire Christians to follow a noble example of repentance, love, devotion, and virtue. For example, Gregory associates the seven demons in Mary Magdalene with the seven deadly sins but then goes on to show how each of these vices had been turned into virtue through her repentance and her following of Christ. One might not be convinced by Gregory's linking the unnamed sinner with Mary Magdalene. But to say Gregory's interpretation was part of a malicious plot to slander Mary Magdalene misses his point entirely. Gregory holds up Mary Magdalene as a model for repentance. And the Church's memory of Mary Magdalene has not emphasized her sins or supposed prostitution. The emphasis has always been on celebrating her conversion, her love for Jesus, and her being the first witness to the Resurrection.

73. ***The Da Vinci Code* says Jesus was married to Mary Magdalene, and that this is "a matter of historical record." Is this true?**

In the thousands of pages written by the early Christians, there is not a single text that says Jesus was married to Mary Magdalene. Not in the New Testament gospels. Not in the letters of Paul. Not in the Church Fathers. Not even in the Gnostic gospels!

All the evidence points in the other direction: that Jesus was not married at all. For example, if Jesus did have a wife, the gospels certainly had many opportunities to tell us about it. Although they often tell us about Jesus' relatives (his father, mother, cousins), they never mention a wife. This seems quite odd if Jesus really had been married.

Furthermore, Mary Magdalene is never mentioned as "the wife of Jesus" in the New Testament. Women in the gospels are often associated with the significant men who are close to them, if in fact there were such men in their lives. What's striking is that Mary Magdalene's name is often listed with the names of other women who are linked with the well-known men in their lives, such as "Mary "[Jesus'] mother" (John 19:25), "Mary the wife of Clopas" (John 19:25), and "Johanna the wife of Chuza" (Luke 8:3). Yet, the thing that stands out about Mary Magdalene is that whenever her name is mentioned, she is often identified with her hometown of Magdala, but never with any man. In other words, she is never introduced as "Mary the wife of ...," but just "Mary Magdalene." This small detail speaks volumes. It indicates that Mary Magdalene was not married at all, much less married to Jesus Christ.

Finally, none of the other Christian writers in the early Church, not even the Gnostic gospels themselves, report that Jesus was married to Mary Magdalene.

74. The Gnostic *Gospel of Philip* calls Mary Magdalene the "companion" of Jesus, and *The Da Vinci Code* says that the word "companion" in Aramaic means spouse. Isn't that at least some proof that she was married to Jesus?

The character Teabing does comment on this passage from the *Gospel of Philip*: "As any Aramaic scholar will tell you, the word *companion* in those days meant spouse." But the main problem with Teabing's statement is that the *Gospel of Philip* was not even written in Aramaic! It was written in Coptic, and the word for *companion* used in this passage is actually the Greek term *koinonos*. And *koinonos* does not mean specifically "wife" or "spouse." It simply indicates one whom another has fellowship with, and it covers a broad range of relationships. The word can describe a business partner, a co-worker, or a fellow Christian. It could include family relationships, too, but if the author of the *Gospel of Philip* wanted to specify spouse or wife, another more precise Greek word could have been chosen (*gyne*). It is most likely, then, that the word *koinonos* in this passage is meant to describe Mary Magdalene as a spiritual sister with Christ.

75. **But *The Da Vinci Code* points out that in ancient Jewish culture, celibacy was condemned. So why would Jesus refrain from marriage? Wouldn't celibacy make Him very "un-Jewish"?**

Celibacy was *not* "condemned" in ancient Jewish culture. Certainly, being married and having children was the normal path for most Jewish men—as it is for Christians as well. But in certain circumstances, celibacy was regarded with tremendous respect.

Some of the most revered men in Jewish history refrained from marriage. For example, the prophet Jeremiah was commanded by God to abstain from marriage, and no one accused him of being "un-Jewish" for this. On the contrary, he was held in high esteem as one of the greatest prophets sent by God to the Jewish people (Jeremiah 16:1-2). A Jewish group in the time of Jesus known as the Essenes held up celibacy as an ideal for its members, many of whom lived unmarried lives in a monastic-like community near the Dead Sea. These members were not criticized for their celibacy but were highly respected for this pious practice by others in the Jewish world. From the biblical evidence, John the Baptist seems to have lived an unmarried life, as did Paul, the former zealous Pharisee, who advocates celibacy as a religious ideal for those who can remain single-minded for the Lord (see 1 Corinthians 7). Therefore, while celibacy was not common in first century Judaism, it was not unheard of, and it certainly wasn't looked down upon, outlawed, or condemned. As we have seen, it was highly esteemed in some individuals.

76. **According to *The Da Vinci Code*, the Gnostic *Gospel of Philip* goes on to say Jesus loved Mary Magdalene more than all the other disciples and "used to kiss her often on her mouth." Doesn't this clearly show that at least some early Christians believed Jesus and Mary Magdalene had a romantic relationship?**

First, we must note that the *Gospel of Philip* does *not* say Jesus "used to kiss Mary Magdalene often on her mouth." *The Da Vinci Code* is misleading readers on this point. The actual manuscript of the *Gospel of Philip* that was found is not complete but fragmented, and it does not say *where* Jesus kissed her nor *how often* He did this. The fragmented text in question says: "And the companion of the [...] Mary Magdalene [...] loved her more than all the disciples, and used to kiss her [...] on [....]" (Brackets indicate gaps in the manuscript.)

Therefore, the actual manuscript of the *Gospel of Philip* does not say where Jesus kissed Mary Magdalene. It could have been a simple kiss of peace. It could have been a non-sexual kiss on her hand, her forehead, or her cheek. *The Da Vinci Code* misleads readers into thinking the text says Jesus kissed Mary on the mouth, when the text itself is not clear at all on the location of this supposed kiss. Furthermore, for Gnostics, the image of a kiss is not a romantic or sexual gesture. Why? Because Gnostics viewed the soul as imprisoned by the body, and sex was seen as the means through which new souls become imprisoned. So the goal of Gnosic spirituality was liberation from the body and its sensual desires.

For Gnostics, a kiss is a symbol for fellowship between believers and for spiritual nourishment passing from one person to the next. That is why, in another Gnostic document called the *Second Apocalypse of James*, Jesus addresses His cousin James as "My beloved!" and likewise kisses him. The gesture is a non-sexual one intended to show the privileged position of the disciple and his (or her) special status as the recipient of secret wisdom.

So even on its own terms, the *Gospel of Philip* says nothing about Mary Magdalene being married to Jesus. According to this and other Gnostic documents, Mary Magdalene might have had a closer friendship with Jesus than did any of the other apostles, and Mary Magdalene might have had greater insights into the mysteries of Christ's kingdom. But nowhere in the *Gospel of Philip* (or in any of the Gnostic writings) is Mary ever presented as the wife of Jesus or even as having a romantic relationship with Him.

77. Is there any theological reason for Jesus to have remained unmarried?

The fact that Jesus remained unmarried makes a lot of sense, though not because marriage or sex is in any way bad or evil. On the contrary, Catholicism affirms the great dignity of marriage as a sacramental covenant blessed by God. Marriage, indeed, is something very good and holy.

Rather, it makes sense that Jesus would refrain from marrying on earth in order to express more fully His complete union with His Father in heaven, as well as His total attentiveness to His Father's will. Christ's celibacy underscores this in a powerful way: Jesus is totally consecrated to His Father, offering up the entirety of His humanity—even His sexuality in celibacy—as a loving, sacrificial gift to the Father. That Jesus himself recognized exactly that as a reason for celibacy is clear from his own words: "For there are eunuchs who have been so from birth, and there are eunuchs who have been made eunuchs by men, and there are eunuchs who have made themselves eunuchs for the sake of the kingdom of heaven. He who is able to receive this, let him receive it" (Matthew 19:12).

Furthermore, Christ's celibacy also most beautifully expresses His radical love for us. It reminds us that He is our divine Bridegroom who gives Himself completely to His people. Throughout salvation history, many terms are used to describe God's relationship with Israel: Creator, Lord, Father, etc. But the most profound and most intimate image used in the Bible is that of marriage. In the Old Testament, God is described as the Bridegroom, and Israel is His chosen Bride. When Israel is faithful to her covenant with God, she is described as the beautiful, faithful spouse, whom God rescued from slavery in Egypt, wedded on Mount Sinai, and led to the Promised Land. Later in Israel's history, when the people broke their covenant with God and began worshiping other deities, Israel is called an unfaithful wife, an adulteress. Still, the prophets announced that God would remain completely faithful to Israel, even though she had been so unfaithful to Him. The prophets also foretold that one day, God would reunite Himself to His bride, heal her of her impurities, and renew His marriage covenant with her.

So when Jesus comes to bring about this new covenant, He is very appropriately called the Bridegroom (Matthew 9:15; John 3:28-36), fulfilling the messianic prophecies and reuniting Himself to His Bride. The fact that Jesus remained unmarried to any single human being more beautifully expresses the profound reality of His complete, unconditional spousal love for *all* His people in the Church, which the New Testament calls the "bride of Christ" (Ephesians 5:21-33).

78. **If, as *The Da Vinci Code* asserts, neither Jesus nor Mary Magdalene were divine, why would "true Christianity" have been about worshiping her and the "sacred feminine"?**

The Da Vinci Code frequently makes claims that sound shocking but that make no sense when you think about them. This is a good example. There's no point in talking about Jesus' attempt to restore the balance between the "sacred masculine" and the "sacred feminine" if, as the book claims, Jesus and Mary Magdalene were mere mortals that none of His followers worshiped. This is one of the places where

Brown simply contradicts himself and hopes nobody will notice. He achieves this effect by dragging in accusations that the "chauvinistic hierarchy" kept Mary Magdalene down. In an age dominated by conspiracy theories and feminist rhetoric, this claim somehow feels believable even though there is nothing to back it up and it doesn't even make sense.

At the end of the day, Brown is trying to tell us that the really exciting, "true" story is that a dead rabbi had a girlfriend, while the Church covered all this up with the ho-hum tale that this rabbi rose from the dead, was seen by Mary Magdalene, and that this woman became the very first person in the history of the human race to announce the good news that God had met, fought, and beaten all the powers of death.

79. I guess that's why the Church honors Mary Magdalene as "apostle to the apostles."

Right! And venerating Mary Magdalene as a great saint and honoring her as the very first witness of Christ's resurrection and as the "apostle to the apostles" is an awfully odd way of smearing somebody as a prostitute and erasing her from the memory of your followers. Similarly, if the Church was all about showing Peter's superiority to Mary Magdalene, why would it carefully preserve (in all four of the gospels) the horrible image of Peter promising Jesus his eternal fidelity and then promptly denying Him in His hour of crisis? Why show Mary as a lone voice courageously bearing witness to the Resurrection with the apostles doubting her if the whole point of the gospels is to show Mary's inferiority and the apostles' superiority?

CHAPTER 13

BLUNDERS AND LIES ABOUT THE CHURCH AFTER CONSTANTINE

80. What happened after the Council of Nicea?

This is an important question. A major portion of *The Da Vinci Code*'s thesis rests on the idea that "history is a lie agreed upon by the victors." In the book's portrayal of the Catholic Church, the Christian faith is supposedly an artifact that remains behind as a relic of the power of the Emperor Constantine. In essence, Brown claims Constantine needed a god through which he could control people and he found that god in Jesus. So, according to Brown, Constantine engineered the Council of Nicea in order to raise Jesus to divinity, concentrate power in the hands of "the Vatican" (which, as we have pointed out previously, would not exist for centuries), and rule the Empire. We would expect then, that after the Council of Nicea, history consists of the winners at the Council consolidating that great victory.

What we find, however, could almost have been designed to show Brown's extraordinarily bad grasp of history. For the fact is, the bishops at the Council of Nicea had only God to back them up, not the emperor. The interest of the Imperial Court was not so much in Catholic orthodoxy as in maintaining civil peace. So, as the decades rolled on, all the Empire's most powerful people backed not Catholic orthodoxy but the various political compromises favoring the Arian and semi-Arian heresy that the Council had been called to settle.

Arians essentially argued that Jesus, while the greatest of all God's creatures and a sort of "god" to us mere mortals, was not God with a capital "G." To the chattering classes in the late Roman Empire, this seemed to be a much more sensible middle-of-the-road view than the teaching of the Council of Nicea and the Catholic Church. Far from "consolidating power," the Catholic Church found itself as harried and persecuted after Nicea as before. The great champion of the Nicene (i.e., Catholic) view of Jesus, Athanasius, was exiled five times, falsely charged with murder (and only escaped execution when he dramatically produced the alleged "victim" in court), and generally treated badly almost his entire life. In fact, forty years after Nicea, an emperor named Julian arose who grew tired with the whole matter and abandoned the dull Arian Christianity of the Imperial Court altogether. He then attempted to bring back old Roman paganism.

Bottom line: *The Da Vinci Code's* portrayal of the Catholic Church as nothing more than the creation of Constantine is, once again, shoddy history.

81. According to Brown, Christianity after Constantine embarked on a bloody campaign to crush and oppress both women and the sacred feminine, resulting in the murder of five million witches. Is this accurate?

No. The best estimates are that between 30,000 to 50,000 witches of both sexes were killed in witch persecutions, mainly in the late Middle Ages and Renaissance. That means these persecutions took place about a thousand years *after* Constantine and had no connection with him whatsoever. Nor do they have any connection to the Vatican, nor to some sort of systematic Church-wide program of the persecution of women. In three-quarters of Catholic Europe there were no witch persecutions at all. The majority of persecutions that did occur were local events and, as such, were not organized by the pope. In addition, some of the most virulent witch persecutions took place in Protestant Europe and colonial America where the command of the papacy did not exactly count for much.

82. *The Da Vinci Code* calls the *Malleus Maleficarum* the most "blood-soaked" book in human history. What was it?

The Da Vinci Code's claims about the massive campaign allegedly organized by "the Vatican" against feminine spirituality rest in great part on the central role played by a 15th century book called the *Malleus Maleficarum* (meaning "Hammer of Witches"). It is indeed one of the most influential witch-hunting manuals of all time and is responsible for many reprehensible crimes. Yet for all that, its history does not do much for *The Da Vinci Code's* case. Here's why.

The *Malleus Maleficarum* was largely the work of one man: Heinrich Kramer (aka Henry Institoris), a Catholic priest and Inquisitor of Innsbruck, Germany. Far from being deep in Rome's alleged globe-spanning plots and counsels against the "sacred feminine," Kramer was not well-respected. His theories on witchcraft were laughed off by most of his fellow clergymen as grotesque and absurd. In fact, other priests of his day condemned his rather creepy obsessions. The Bishop of Innsbruck became so irritated at Kramer's fascination with the alleged sexual behavior of witches that he shut down Kramer's inquisitions, declaring that the devil was actually in the inquisitor rather than in his defendants (i.e., the alleged witches). These facts are difficult to square with a vast Catholic conspiracy that lionized Kramer.

Remaining undaunted, Kramer did what any good fanatic does: he wrote the *Malleus* to vindicate himself, sort of like self-proclaimed UFO abductees who publish long websites full of blurry pictures to "prove" their claims to a skeptical world. In other words, the *Malleus Maleficarum* was hardly a papal blueprint for suppression of the "sacred feminine." It's a minority opinion, written by one odd priest to convince a skeptical majority of the grave dangers of witchcraft.

Kramer then wrangled two coups, the first by luck, the second by lies. First, he complained to the pope about the persecution he was receiving from other priests and persuaded the pope (who, like many in his time, was concerned about witchcraft) to endorse it officially in a document entitled *Summis Desiderantes*. This endorsement shouldn't be seen as particularly significant. One gets the impression the pope was, at best, cautiously supportive, given that he asked a respected Dominican scholar, Jacob Sprenger, to help Kramer revise the *Malleus*.

Kramer, though, treated the pope's letter as a complete stamp of approval. Feeling bolstered, he then proceeded to step two: presenting the *Malleus* to the Faculty of Cologne, the Inquisition's top theologians, asking for their approval. Instead, the Faculty rejected the book outright, declaring that the legal procedures it recommended were unethical and illegal, and that its demonology was inconsistent with Catholic doctrine.

Undaunted, Kramer simply forged a recommendation of the book from the Faculty of Cologne and went on his merry way. This worked until the Faculty discovered the outrage. In 1490, four years after the *Malleus* was published, the Inquisition condemned Kramer. Again, this does not fit very well with *The Da Vinci Code*, which basically alleges that the *Malleus* was a sort of "official Catholic guide to the suppression of women."

Eventually, however, this absurd book, filled with the weird psychosexual musings of a German priest who was condemned by the Catholic Church as a fanatic, a crank, and a forger, became very popular when witch hunting manias later swept both Protestant and Catholic communities. While Church courts ignored it, civil courts began to take it seriously. Fooled by the papal letter and forged Cologne faculty recommendation, non-religious judges thought the *Malleus* was Church-approved, just as non-scholarly readers think *The Da Vinci Code* is "scholar-approved." Indeed, the parallels are, at once, eerie, amusing, and disturbing. Rather like *The Da Vinci Code*, the *Malleus* seemed to many readers to be providing the "inside story" on esoteric spirituality unknown to the unwashed masses. And so, it wound up becoming the "guide" for witch hunters in the 16th century, when various local panics left civil judges casting about for some way to navigate. The *Malleus Maleficarum* did indeed do much evil. But it's pretty hard to blame the Catholic Church, the Vatican, or Constantine for it. And it's particularly difficult for it to be labeled "the most blood-soaked" book in history. Other works, such as the *Communist Manifesto* and *Mein Kampf* laid out plans that sent tens of millions to their deaths.

CHAPTER 14

MASCULINE AND FEMININE IN THE BIBLE

83. Isn't it unfair that God should be depicted with masculine imagery in the Bible? Scripture does pretty much claim that God is male, doesn't it?

Actually, no. The Bible makes it exceedingly clear that God is neither male nor female; He is a Spirit. Remember: it is paganism—not the Catholic faith or the Bible—that sees God as simply an expansion on whatever bit of Nature we happen to fancy. In contrast, the Catholic faith sees Nature as a dim reflection of a God who is utterly transcendent. Because of this, God is the source of *both* masculinity and femininity. While God is neither male nor female, both masculinity and femininity reflect attributes of God. For this reason, the book of Genesis describes the creation of human beings this way: "So God created man in his own image, in the image of God he created him; *male and female he created them*" (Genesis 1:27).

The full image of God is not simply man but man and woman together. Of course, God is, in Himself, beyond the distinctions of human gender. We refer to God as "Him" rather than "It" because God is a *person* (in fact, *three* Persons, the Trinity); He is not some impersonal "force" or "energy."

84. Then why does Christianity constantly address God in masculine terms as "Father," "Lord," and so forth?

Precisely because the Bible itself has revealed Him in this way. It was, after all, Jesus who taught "When you pray, say: 'Father'" (Luke 11:2). God reveals Himself as "Father" because this best describes His relationship with Jesus, His Son, and with us. This, of course, does not mean "men are superior to women." In terms of dignity, male and female are absolutely equal. As Paul states, in Christ Jesus, "There is neither Jew nor Greek, there is neither slave nor free, there is neither male nor female; for you are all one in Christ Jesus" (Galatians 3:28).

But saying men and women are *equal in dignity* is entirely different from saying that they are the *same*. In addition to Paul's teaching, we know from common sense that they are not. There is a natural complementarity between masculine and feminine. The masculine initiates, the feminine responds. As the sky (and pagan sky "gods") pour in light and seed and energy, so the earth (and the earth goddesses of paganism) respond with fruitfulness and life. This insight, which paganism captures in its myths, is not denied but brought to fullness in the revelation of Christ. That is why Christ is called the "Bridegroom" and the Church is called the "Bride" (see Ephesians, chapter 5). The "sacred feminine" is indeed part of Catholic and Christian teaching. Only it does not mean that we worship goddesses. It means that the holy Church that Christ founded is joined to Him in love by the Holy Spirit and is made a participant in His divine nature by His self-donating sacrifice and resurrection. The great model of this—and the "elephant in the living room" Brown overlooks in his claims about the Catholic Church's supposed hatred of the "sacred feminine"—is the Blessed Virgin Mary, Jesus' first and greatest disciple. If the Catholic Church hates the sacred feminine, why all the Marian devotion?

85. So the Catholic Church doesn't teach that God is male?

No. The Church teaches that the masculine (which initiates, fertilizes, and energizes) and the feminine (which responds, contemplates, and brings forth life) are to be found in God Himself. This is why only male and female together fully image God as Genesis teaches. The Father pours out His life to the Son. The Son gives back to the Father all the life and love the Father has given Him. And from this communion of love proceeds the Holy Spirit like the harmonic in a musical chord—the Third Person of the Blessed Trinity. God is, if you will, a sort of eternal "holy family": three persons in One God.

86. If God is both masculine and feminine, then isn't Brown right to say that we should worship both gods and goddesses?

No. We should worship God. Gods and goddesses are not God. They are our bad crayon drawings of God. They are God made in our own image, not vice versa. They become our replacements for God. Remember the blunder of paganism: the mistake of worshiping creatures instead of the Creator. Far and away the easiest creatures to worship are the ones we invent ourselves, because it is very easy to adore the work of our hands and to create "gods" who tell us what we want to hear rather than the truth. God instead commands us to worship Him alone, since He alone is God and truly worthy of worship. God has made it possible for us to do this by giving us not simply a picture of Himself, but Himself in the form of a human being: Jesus Christ. In Jesus, God Himself became man, took upon Himself the sins of the world, died, and rose again so that we could participate in the divine life of the Blessed Trinity. It was He, not Constantine or the apostles, who founded the Catholic Church to be His Bride. In other words, Jesus really does take the "sacred feminine" seriously. Much more seriously than Dan Brown, in fact. Brown sees the "sacred feminine" as a kind of religious affirmative action program so that we can add a few goddesses to the starting lineup of gods.

Jesus, though, reveals the truth: God is not a product of our imagination. Rather, we are products of God's imagination. So the way in which God reveals Himself to us matters. And a profound aspect of that revelation is that God is masculine in relation to the whole human race just as the human race is feminine in relation to God. God comes to share His life with us—His Bride, the Church—and make us participants in His divine nature (2 Peter 1:4). Brown has it backward. He thinks the point of the divine is sex: thus, Jesus had an earthly wife. In reality, the point of sex is the Divine. All our earthly experiences of marriage are a foreshadowing of the Great Marriage: the Wedding Feast of the Christ the Bridegroom and

His Bride the Church (Ephesians 5; Revelation 22) in heaven. This mistake of reversing Creator and creation is the essence of paganism.

87. But Langdon talks about the divine order of Nature. Surely that's not an attack on the Church?

It all depends on what Langdon means by the "divine order" of Nature. Brown falls into semireligious cadences in his writing that are meant to give the impression that his hero is not hostile to "true spirituality" but instead is "deeply spiritual." And since most modern people figure that one "deeply spiritual" person is pretty much the same as another, they assume that Brown isn't really attacking "authentic Christianity" but simply the corruptions that have flowed from misunderstanding "the true message of Jesus."

This is, however, quite false. For true "spirituality" is not a mood or a poetic sounding turn of phrase. Spirituality has to do with spirit—most particularly, the Spirit of God. Jesus did not teach us some fuzzy notion that Nature is divine or identical to God. He knows that Nature is the *creation* of God because He is God and was "present at the Creation." Nature has a divine order—not because it is divine but because its divine Creator has given it that order.

88. So you're saying that everything depends on where the divine order in Nature comes from and where it points us to?

Exactly. Paul the apostle sums things up by pointing out that Nature is indeed divinely ordered and that this order points us, not to Nature, but to the reality of the divine Creator:

> For what can be known about God is plain to them, because God has shown it to them. Ever since the creation of the world his invisible nature, namely, his eternal power and deity, has been clearly perceived in the things that have been made. So they are without excuse. (Romans 1:19-20)

Paul then continues and points out clearly the mistake of paganism by describing the fundamental blunder of worshiping the orderly creation rather than the Creator:

> For although they knew God they did not honor him as God or give thanks to him, but they became futile in their thinking and their senseless minds were darkened. Claiming to be wise, they became fools, and exchanged the glory of the immortal God for images resembling mortal man or birds or animals or reptiles. (Romans 1:21-23)

This is precisely what Brown is calling his readers to do: worship creatures such as Mary Magdalene rather than the Creator. And this is precisely what we know Jesus repudiated because we know He was a devout Jew who taught His disciples to keep the commandments, including, especially "You shall worship the Lord your God and him only shall you serve" (Matthew 4:10). In other words, *The Da Vinci Code* is promoting a corruption of Jesus' teaching by radically departing from the Bible.

CHAPTER 15

CHRISTIANITY AND THE "PAGAN CONNECTION"

89. I'm a bit puzzled. Sometimes the characters in *The Da Vinci Code* seem to be saying that paganism is good because of the "sacred feminine." But, at other times, they seem upset with Christianity because it's really just warmed over paganism.

You're right. *The Da Vinci Code's* main characters—especially Langdon and Teabing—spend a fair amount of time making a number of mutually contradictory claims in a kind of verbal shell game.

First, they try to tell us Constantine was the mastermind who changed the worldview of antiquity from matriarchal paganism to patriarchal Christianity. On this accounting, pre-Christian paganism was a monolithic bloc of goddess worshipers, which is about as sensible as saying "sports fans" all root for the same team, or even the same sport. In fact, as we have already seen, "pagan" simply refers to "people who do not worship the God of Abraham"; the term covers every belief system from Greco-Roman religion, to the Hindu pantheon, to Eastern philosophers who can scarcely be spoken of as worshiping anything at all. A pagan could worship Venus, Mithras, Apollo, Ashtoreth, Horus, Quetzalcoatl, the nearest tree, the

Force—or all of them, or none of them. The notion that a given pagan necessarily even *cares* about the "sacred feminine" is by no means certain.

But according to *The Da Vinci Code*, Constantine is guilty of "waging a campaign of propaganda that demonized the sacred feminine, obliterating the goddess from modern religion forever." So Christianity is evil because it allegedly wiped out all that jolly paganism that was happily worshiping the goddess.

Then, in a classic contradiction, they argue that Christianity is also the product of a pagan Constantine who converted "sun-worshiping pagans to Christianity" by ingeniously mingling paganism and the Jesus sect into a "hybrid religion." So Christianity is actually pagan and not really about Christ at all.

And then, in a final burst of incoherence, they assert that not only is Christianity really just warmed-over paganism that uncritically accepts whatever was current in pagan culture, it is also profoundly intolerant of paganism. After all, it launched a "smear campaign" against pagan gods, "recasting their divine symbols as evil ... In the battle between the pagan symbols and the Christian symbols, the pagans lost." So Christianity is *also* evil because it is actually not pagan but is intolerantly Christian.

So, according to Brown, all pagans were goddess worshipers before the pagan Constantine—who took paganism and used it to attack goddess worship and invent Christianity—which is nothing but paganism that fiercely rejects paganism. Makes your head spin, doesn't it? Obviously, logical consistency is not a fundamental characteristic of *The Da Vinci Code.*

90. That may be so, but what about all those pagan parallels between Christianity and other ancient religions?

The discussion of pagan parallels with the Christian faith is actually quite old. Some medieval Christians, for instance, were struck by the fact that pre-Christian philosophers, poets, and mystery cults sometimes bore a curious, fleeting resemblance to the prophets of the Old Testament. Michelangelo goes so far as to decorate the Sistine Chapel not merely with the prophets of the Old Testament, but also with Greek sibyls and oracles. In short, the notion that elements of pagan religious culture resemble the Christian revelation is not a discovery of Dan Brown.

The real question, of course, is what does this resemblance mean? Brown takes it as a foregone conclusion that it means everything in Christianity was simply stolen from paganism. Upon further investigation, though, this assumption falls apart.

For instance, Brown declares it significant that the use of the "halo" in Christian art (i.e., to symbolize holiness or divinity) resembles Egyptian sun disks, as though the association of luminosity and divine wisdom could only occur to an Egyptian and must have been "stolen" by Christians. But this is like saying that the apostle Paul stole the idea of walking around on two legs from Aristotle or that Jesus borrowed the notion of eating supper with His friends from Socrates.

What all these "strange coincidence" theories ignore is that some religious ideas are as universal as broad daylight. That's why a Hebrew psalmist could describe the Lord God as a sun and a shield (Psalm 84:11) while Greeks could associate divine splendor with the sun in the figure of Apollo, Pharaoh Akhenaton could mistake the sun for God, and Jesus could call Himself the Light of the World. It's just not that hard to associate light that illumines the eye with truth that illumines the mind. Every normal human makes that association, including atheistic philosophers of the 18th century who proclaimed themselves "Enlightened" while refusing to worship Ra, Apollo, or Jesus Christ.

91. So the use of pagan imagery doesn't mean Christianity is really pagan in origin?

Right. It simply means that God uses human things to communicate truth. It's not strange, therefore, to see the gospel writers employing such obvious motifs as light or water or sacred meals to express life in Jesus Christ. What would be very strange—even incomprehensible—is if Christians *had not* done this. Christianity teaches its followers that there is one God who is the Author of all truth, beauty, and goodness. If a Christian who truly believed this were to encounter the truths in Aristotelian philosophy, the beauties in Egyptian art, or the goodness of sunlight, it would be very strange for him to *refuse* to allow anything about them into Christian life on the grounds that doing so would "corrupt" Christianity. One may as well argue that a modern minister must worship Greek gods if he illustrates a sermon with one of *Aesop's Fables*.

92. But what about the really disturbing similarities between Christianity and paganism, such as the similarities between Mithras and Christ?

When it comes to Mithras, the question Brown never quite gets around to discussing is just who is borrowing from whom. Brown notes a number of similarities between Mithras worship and Christianity. What he does not tell you is that Mithras worship is a phenomenon that likely borrows from Christianity, not vice versa. There is no record of it as a popular cult throughout the Roman Empire until *after* the establishment of Christianity.

Even in practices where Christianity does borrow from pre-Christian paganism (e.g., Christmas trees, holly and ivy, Easter eggs, wedding rings) the question is, "What does Christianity do with these things?" The only problem would be if Christianity took pagan forms and gave them a pagan meaning: for instance, encouraging Christians to throw out the worship of the God of Israel and replace it with the adoration of Druidic nature gods. But Christianity has never done this. Instead, it has taken pagan forms and filled them with Christian content.

So, mere parallels with paganism mean nothing by themselves and often serve to demonstrate the exact opposite of what *The Da Vinci Code* claims.

93. *The Da Vinci Code* seems to spend a huge amount of time talking about sex. Why is this?

A major theme of *The Da Vinci Code* is the deification of sex. Remember the definition of paganism: worshiping the creature instead of the Creator. In essence, Brown is advocating the worship of sex (remember Saunière's participation in the rite of *Hieros Gamos?*). So instead of seeing our earthly experiences of sex and gender as pointing to the cosmic truths about Christ the Bridegroom and His Bride the Church, or recognizing in our sexual nature a dim reflection of the masculine and feminine that find their roots in the very being of the Blessed Trinity in whose image we are created, *The Da Vinci Code* gets it exactly backward. It portrays the whole Christian religion as the cover-up for a naughty little sexual affair between a dead rabbi and his girlfriend. The book then blows up this affair to become the basis for an entirely new "church" founded on the "sacred feminine" centering on a cult honoring that girlfriend. In other words, Brown's big idea is that we should worship sex or, more precisely, the sexes. Since we live in an era that is obsessed with sex, his version of Christ has, for the moment, become the latest "real" Jesus.

CHAPTER 16

HOW *THE DA VINCI CODE* PREYS UPON THE HISTORICALLY IGNORANT

94. What do you mean by the "latest real Jesus"?

The basic rule of thumb to use whenever one encounters a brand new "real Jesus" who is trendy yet radically at odds with the ordinary teaching of the Church is this: *Every new "real Jesus" reveals far more about us than it does about Him.*

That's why, when liberal Protestantism got overly excited about the Social Gospel a hundred years ago, the new "real Jesus" looked very much like a Social Gospel Protestant *a la* Albert Schweitzer. When the world became enamored with Marxism, another "real Jesus" suddenly appeared on the scene as the first Marxist preaching the Sermon on the Barricades to the Oppressed Proletariat. In the 1920s, when big business was booming in the United States, Jesus suddenly was discovered by American author Bruce Barton to be "the founder of modern business" in his book *The Man Nobody Knows* which portrayed Jesus as the Super Salesman. In the 1930s, Nazism promoted a "real Jesus" who was "really" an Aryan with no connection to Judaism. In the 1960s and 1970s, Jesus morphed into a Flower Child in *Godspell* and a Rock God in *Jesus*

Christ Superstar. In the 1980s, New Age "prophets" discovered a "real Jesus" who offered the same sort of "get rich and heal your inner child" twaddle they offered. In the 1990s, gay rights advocates suddenly found a homosexual Jesus in the blasphemous play *Corpus Christi.*

In our time, we live in a popular, celebrity-obsessed culture that's fascinated with the sex lives (real and imagined) of the rich and famous. We also live in an age that has seen the rise of feminism and that prizes something called "spirituality"—an amorphous New Age benevolence that affirms us in our "okayness." But though we love spirituality, we loathe religion and the thought of a transcendent Father God who might bother us with commands, "thou shalt nots," and "sin." And finally, we live in the post-Watergate age of the *X-Files,* in which vast conspiracies by sinister organizations are widely credited with little critical thought.

That's just what The *Da Vinci Code* tries to sell us: a new "real Jesus" with an active sex life who is all about "sacred feminine" paganism with its duality of god and goddess—and who is, naturally, hushed up by the big bad Church whose God is typically spoken of using the scary pronoun "He."

95. What is Wicca and neo-paganism?

Wicca is a made-up religion that was concocted about fifty years ago by Gerald Brosseau Gardner, under the pretense that it was the original, matriarchal, nature religion of Europe that held sway before the arrival of Christianity. Similar to Plantard's phony "Priory of Sion," Wicca claims to have connections to "deep history" when in fact it was essentially created out of whole cloth after World War II. It claims that it was driven underground during "the Burning Times," that vague period during which the Church supposedly began to kill all the female keepers of the ancient flame of "sacred feminine" paganism. It has grown in popularity because it is a very convenient fiction for people who wish to replace Christianity with a sort of pagan feminist myth.

96. Why should I believe the official Christian version of history rather than *The Da Vinci Code's*?

Because the Christian version has evidence for it—evidence even accepted by non-believers—while *The Da Vinci Code's* version of history is entirely baseless. It is, in fact, precisely what Brown claims the Christian story to be: a fiction invented in order to support an ideology, full of events that did not happen (such as the marriage of Jesus, Constantine making Jesus into God, and five million witches murdered by order of the Vatican). History is the record of events that actually happened. Many secular historians have commented that the vast majority of *The Da Vinci Code's* historical claims are distortions or complete fabrications.

97. Brown talks about three centuries of persecution after Constantine and links it with the *Malleus Maleficarum*. But the two are separated by more than a thousand years. What gives?

What gives, again, is the fact that Brown is not interested in fact, but in creating the impression that the primary purpose of the Catholic faith is to oppress women and to stamp out the "sacred feminine." So he says whatever it takes and hopes that the reader will not notice the absurdity of his historical claims. The reality is that the *Malleus Maleficarum* is the work of people living more than a thousand years after Constantine. The notion that Constantine has some program in mind that resulted in the publication of the *Malleus* is just one more example of the astonishingly shoddy research behind *The Da Vinci Code*.

CHAPTER 17

IF *THE DA VINCI CODE* IS FALSE, THEN WHAT?

98. So if Jesus was not just "a mortal prophet, a great and powerful man" as *The Da Vinci Code* claims, then who was He?

You have just put your finger on the central question of the Gospel. And it is asked by none other than Jesus Himself, who turned to His disciples and said: "Who do you say I am?" The case for Christ rests on the various claims people have made in response to that question. For there are really only *five possibilities*, and they all start with the letter "L."*

Jesus was either:

A) a **legend**—that is, He never really existed; the New Testament is just a fable.

B) a **liar**—in effect, He didn't really mean the things He said. He was simply trying to pull a fast one on the people for personal gain.

C) a **lunatic**—that is, His claims to be God were merely the ranting of a crazy mind.

D) a **light and fluffy New Ager**—that is, He was trying to tell us we are all gods.

*Note: This answer is adapted from "The Case for Christ" in *A Guide to the Passion* (Ascension Press, 2004).

E) the **Lord**—He was who He claimed to be: the Son of God, the Messiah, God Incarnate.

Now, let's examine each of these possibilities:

A) Jesus was just a **legend**.

The problem with calling Jesus a "legend" is that no reputable historian in the world would say Jesus never existed. We know when the documents of the New Testament were written. As was discussed previously, most of the New Testament was written when the eyewitnesses to the events of Jesus' life, death, and resurrection were still alive. And the telling thing about not only the authors, but also the people who preserved their writings over the centuries, is how little interest they seem to have had in "adjusting" history in order to create a legend.

Think about it: If the apostles were enthusiasts who just got a bit excited and mistook their rabbi for God, then why do the Gospel accounts show the disciples to be slow to understand His message and put their faith in Him?

Clearly we are looking at neither theological rocket scientists nor overly spiritual hysterics. In fact, the biblical documents continually paint a picture of the apostles as men who were a little slow on the uptake, as rather typically ambitious, and as cowards who abandoned the one they loved at the moment of His supreme crisis (Mark 14:50). It's highly unlikely that these men "puffed up" the story of Jesus for their own personal gain. Think about it: If you wanted to start your own new religious movement—touting the wonders of your leader—would you realistically show your leader in a negative light?

Followers who are trying to burnish the historical record and turn a mere human rabbi into a god would not be likely to carefully preserve Christ's last words: "My God, My God, why have you forsaken me?" (Matthew 27:46; Mark 15:34). Nor would they allow the editing scissors to miss quotes such as: "Why do you call me good?' said Jesus, 'No one is good—except God alone' "(Mark 10:18); "He could do no mighty work there, except that he laid his hands upon a few sick people and healed them" (Mark 6:5); and "Who was it that touched me?" (Luke 8:45). Such quotes appear, at first glance, to bear witness to Jesus' imperfection, weakness, and ignorance—not what you want when you are inventing a god.

So if the people who wrote (and preserved) the gospels were not religious maniacs, cultists, liars, fact-fudgers, or historical revisionists, what were they? How about honest men? And these honest men tell us something astonishing: Jesus claimed to be God.

B) Jesus was a **liar**.

OK, so maybe the apostles told what they believed to be true. Isn't it still possible that *Jesus* was the deceiver here? Maybe He was just a clever huckster bent on selling Himself to the crowd for the usual reasons of power and money.

Problem is, Jesus does not do the things that a deceiver or opportunist would do. He flees into the desert when people try to make Him king (John

6:15). Then He makes speeches (see John 6:25-60) that are guaranteed to offend all but the most die-hard grassroots supporters. He repeatedly conceals His miracles (Mark 5:43; 7:36; Luke 5:14). He hobnobs with thieves, drunkards, and lepers. He surrounds Himself with tacky people who would look terrible in campaign brochures. He looks past the president of the Capernaum Chamber of Commerce and, without excusing Himself, extends a cheery "Hello!" to a local prostitute who just crashed the exclusive cocktail party without an invitation (Luke 7:36-50). That's not the way to win political favor. Nor does it make sense to take particular pains to make sure that those Roman and Jewish leaders who thought the least of Him—and had the power to do something about it—would find plenty of reasons (and opportunities) to see Him dead.

Such political "blunders" characterized His entire career. He regularly alienated the most powerful men of His day, both Jewish and Roman:

Again the high priest asked him, "Are you the Christ, the Son of the Blessed?" "I am," [said Jesus] (Mark 14:61-62).

And Pilate asked Him, "Are you the King of the Jews?" And [Jesus] answered him, "You have said so" (Mark 15:2).

He was not a man to quibble about what the meaning of "is" is. Instead, when He was on trial for His life, twice He said the very thing that would absolutely ensure He suffered an ignominious and horrible death. If He was after worldly power, He had a strange way of showing it.

C) Jesus was a **lunatic**.

Well then, perhaps Jesus was just insane and merely believed He was God.

This explanation doesn't work. Consider the Sermon on the Mount in Matthew, chapters 5-7. Does this look to you like the ravings of a lunatic? Read again His deft answer to the people who wanted to catch Him in His words (Mark 12:13-17). Observe the brilliance and subtlety of His answer to those who wanted to stone the woman taken in adultery (John 8:1-11). This kind of savvy is hardly evidence of madness. No wonder people who tried to trick Him were "marveling at his answer [and] they were silent" (Luke 20:26). His lucidity, sense of perspective, irony, and humor do not bespeak madness but great sanity. Nor does even His iron resolve to meet His fate look like madness. We never get the impression that He *desires* death; instead He believes Himself to be commanded by God the Father to overcome death by giving His life "as a ransom for all" (1 Timothy 2:6).

D) Jesus was a **light and fluffy New Ager.**

Well, yes, say some, Jesus *did* claim to be God. But He meant it in an Eastern or "New Age" way. He was merely asserting His "God consciousness" in an attempt to awaken this same consciousness in us. He was, in short, a guru to the Jewish people. When He says He is the Son of God, He means we are *all* children of God and, indeed, we are God ourselves if we but realize it.

It's an interesting thought, but it's not what Jesus said. On the contrary, He affirms that God is *Lord* of heaven and earth, not that He *is* heaven and earth. Indeed, He does not speak of God as identical with Creation; He speaks of Him in a thoroughly Jewish sense as Transcendent Creator, Judge, and Father (Matthew 19:4; 6:14-15). He does not tell His disciples they are parts of God; He plainly reminds them they are sinners in need of salvation who are, apart from Him alone, incapable of accomplishing that salvation or anything else (John 15:5). Far from affirming that He's OK and we're OK, He frequently tells us we are evil, but He is without sin; we are from below, but He is from above (John 8:1-11; 8:23). He insists that the way to life is not by discovering our divinity but by putting our faith exclusively in Him.

Very well then, if the records are reliable they clearly show us a man who is neither merely nice, nor a liar, nor insane, nor a New Age guru. Yet He still stands before us implacably asking, "Who do you say that I am?" (Matthew 16:15). And as He does so in an ever more insistent voice, we begin to feel the grip of C.S. Lewis' logic that:

> The historical difficulty of giving for the life, sayings, and influence of Jesus any explanation that is not harder than the Christian explanation is very great. The discrepancy between the depth and sanity and (let me add) shrewdness of his moral teaching and the rampant megalomania which must lie behind his theological teaching unless He is indeed God, has never been satisfactorily got over. (C.S. Lewis, *Miracles*)

E) Jesus is the **Lord**.

As we consider all the evidence, there is only one possibility that truly satisfies: Jesus is who He says

He is. He is God in the flesh. He is the eternal Son of God, the Messiah, sent to save the world from its sins. He indeed is the Lord of the Universe, who came to give us eternal life. He really and truly shed His blood for us on the cross and He really and truly rose from the dead and ascended into heaven. Now He offers us all the riches of His love, mercy, forgiveness, joy, power, and peace by the gift of the Holy Spirit, and eternal life with His Father through the sacraments of His Church, which is His body.

That's what we find when we really "seek the truth."

99. **Does the upcoming movie version of *The Da Vinci Code* tone down any of the book's outrageous claims?**

Apparently not. Though the $125 million film (set to be released worldwide on May 19, 2006) is still in post-production, its famous director, Ron Howard, has stated in interviews that the screenplay adheres closely to the book and does not "water down" any of the story's more controversial elements. Starring Oscar-winner Tom Hanks (*Forrest Gump*) as Robert Langdon, French actress Audrey Tautou (*Amelie*) as Sophie Neveu, Sir Ian McKellan (*Lord of the Rings*) as Leigh Teabing, Paul Bettany (*A Beautiful Mind*) as Silas, Jean Reno (*The Professional*) as Bezu Fache, and Alfred Molina (*Spiderman 2*) as Bishop Aringarosa, the film is sure to be one of the year's biggest blockbusters—and will undoubtedly do much to spread the book's distorted and erroneous claims to a wider audience.

100. What can Christians do to respond to *The Da Vinci Code*?

Informed Christians have nothing to fear from *The Da Vinci Code*'s many bogus and easily refutable claims. Rather, we should regard its popularity as an opportunity to study our Faith and proclaim it to others.

First, study the Faith: It's true that *The Da Vinci Code* has many outlandish claims, as we've seen throughout the questions and answers in this book. And we could easily write off many of its points right from the start. But let's not settle for responding to our friends and relatives by simply saying, "The book is heresy!" or "These ideas are crazy!" or "You shouldn't be reading that book!" Let's take time to study our Faith and learn more about the Bible itself, especially about how the books came to be and how we know the Scriptures are reliable documents. Let's take time to read about Church history and see the splendor of the Catholic Church as the Church of Jesus Christ, founded on the apostles and used by God to triumphantly transform the pagan Roman world. Let's take time to learn the biblical and historical roots of the Catholic sacraments, rituals, devotions, and doctrines. The more we know about our Faith, the better equipped we will be to share it with others in an intelligent and convincing manner. Visit the Da Vinci Outreach website at www.DaVinciOutreach.com (or www.DaVinciAntidote.com) for free, downloadable resources.

Second, proclaim the Faith: Oddly enough, people in the secular culture are more interested in religion now because of their fascination with the religious themes in *The Da Vinci Code*. From TV interview shows and news documentaries, to conversations at airports, business offices, and dinner parties, people are talking about *The Da Vinci Code*. Their vision of Christianity may be very skewed by the book, but their interest may at least be a doorway into a conversation about religion that would not have been open before. Encourage your priests to address this topic in their homilies—people will be all ears. Offer a discussion group about *The Da Vinci Code* at your parish. Have the priest or religious education director—or perhaps even yourself—give a short talk or lead a discussion. You'll be surprised how many people will show up. Here's another creative idea: One youth minister recently said that instead of simply discouraging high school students from reading the book or seeing the movie, he was going to use all the fanfare as a teaching opportunity for his youth. His plan was to have the youth read short excerpts from *The Da Vinci Code* at their weekly meeting. Each night, *he* was going to play the role of attacking Christianity with the ideas from *The Da Vinci Code* and he was going to challenge *the youth* wrestle with its claims. With his guidance and teaching, these youth then would be led to discover more deeply the beauty of Catholicism: where the Bible came from, the trustworthiness of the Scriptures, the beauty of sacred art, the goodness of the Popes and the Vatican, the richness of the Catholic sacraments, rituals and devotions, and the historical underpinnings of the Catholic faith as seen in Church history.

The Da Vinci Code is, at the end of the day, more of an opportunity than a threat. God orders all things for the good of those who love Christ and are called according to His purposes. As God has always done, He will turn this latest attack on the gospel of His Son into a chance for his truth and love to prevail by mean of the very instruments intended to put Him to death. Just as the cross was turned into the means of our salvation, so God by His divine paradox, will use the frauds, falsehoods, and fallacies to throw into stark relief the plain daylight and common sense of the gospel of Jesus Christ, still faithfully preserved in His one, holy, catholic, and apostolic Church.

ABOUT THE AUTHORS

Mark Shea is senior content editor for Catholic Exchange (www.CatholicExchange.com) and the author of several books, including *Making Senses Out of Scripture: Reading the Bible as the First Christians Did* (Basilica, 1999) and *By What Authority? An Evangelical Discovers Catholic Tradition* (Our Sunday Visitor, 1996). He lives near Seattle with his wife and four sons.

Edward Sri, S.T.D., is assistant professor of theology at Benedictine College in Atchison, Kansas. He is the author of several books, including *The New Rosary in Scripture: Biblical Insights for Praying the 20 Mysteries* (Servant, 2003). Sri is a founding leader with Curtis Martin of FOCUS (Fellowship of Catholic University Students), and he writes and speaks on Scripture, apologetics, and the Catholic faith. He resides in Kansas with his wife Elizabeth and their three children.

Acknowledgments

The authors wish to thank the many people who offered their prayers and encouragement for this project. *Edward Sri:* Richard White, my students at Benedictine College, and most especially, my wife, Elizabeth. I am also grateful to Curtis Mitch, a longtime friend, for his very helpful input. *Mark Shea:* my wife, Janet.

Many thanks also to Bill Donaghy, for his review of the manuscript and helpful suggestions; Annamarie Adkins, Christopher Cope, Michael Flickinger, Michael Fontecchio, Thomas A. Szyszkiewicz, and Karen Zahradka, for their editorial and technical assistance; and Devin Schadt, for his cover design.

BULK DISCOUNTS AVAILABLE!

To place a bulk order of *The Da Vinci Deception*,
call 800.376.0520 or visit
www.DavinciOutreach.com

DAVINCI
OUTREACH

Join **Da Vinci Outreach** as we spread the truth about Jesus Christ and the history of Christianity. We have compiled several excellent resources to help you quickly and effectively get this message out to friends, family, parishioners and anyone whose faith may be adversely affected by the blasphemous claims in *The Da Vinci Code*.

An extremely effective and cost-efficient way to spread the truth about *The Da Vinci Code* is to sponsor your own parish. Parish sponsors purchase *The Da Vinci Deception* at very low bulk discounts, and distribute them in the vestibule of the Church.

At times like this it is crucial for Catholics to stand up for the truth, while the name of Our Lord is being trampled upon by so many. Spreading *The Da Vinci Deception* to members of your parish is the perfect way to innoculate them against the spiritual poison found in *The Da Vinci Code*.

We have free study guides available for high school and adult faith formation levels, as well as parish and group action plans.

www.DavinciOutreach.com

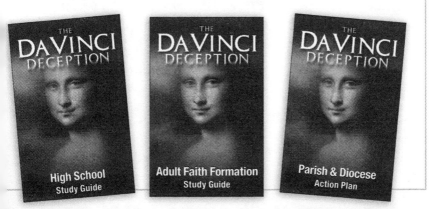

BEFORE YOU STUDY THE BIBLE, UNDERSTAND "THE BIG PICTURE"

Schedule a *Great Adventure* seminar or use our <u>new</u> video series and study guides at your parish!

The *Great Adventure Bible Timeline* is the perfect tool to help you study the Bible. Developed by Jeff Cavins and Tim Gray, the new *Great Adventure* helps people see the "big picture" of Scripture so they can better understand the people, places and events of salvation history. The study of the Bible comes alive when people experience these videos or our live seminar.

To order materials or schedule a seminar, call 800-376-0520 or visit www.TheBibleTimeline.com

JEFF CAVINS

KRISTINE FRANKLIN

SARAH CHRISTMYER

TIM GRAY

EDWARD SRI, PH.D.

TIMELINE TEACHERS

Keep *your passion* for Christ alive by learning the Bible with Catholic Scripture Study.

Catholic Scripture Study (CSS), written by leading Catholic Scripture scholars Scott Hahn and Mark Shea and long available on CatholicExchange.com, is now available in a Group Study Program. Launched in 2003, participating groups around the country and overseas are raving about this powerful, life-changing Bible Study.

In addition to the in-depth and solidly Catholic Bible study and commentaries, CSS now offers a popular classroom format that fosters real learning and true Christian fellowship. Catholics no longer have to stray from the Church to find a vibrant Bible Study!

For more information, please email us:
info@CatholicScriptureStudy.com

or visit:
www.CatholicScriptureStudy.com